nal or organism that eats all things,
her animal or vegetable sources

OMNIVORE

Jim Brisby & Simon Woods

signifi
nutritic
sustain

Introduction – Jim Brisby

Cranswick celebrates its 50th anniversary this year and I've been part of the company for 30 of those years. Over these five decades, despite rising living standards and global supply chains making food more affordable, our diets have not improved. In the UK, we now spend less than 10% of our income on food, one of the lowest rates globally.

Our diets barely changed for millennia and historically were based on local, seasonal, freshly prepared food. It is only in recent decades that food has become globalised, industrialised and more processed.

My father and grandfather were both farmers, my grandfather on a modest mixed farm of arable, beef cattle, sheep and chickens and my father producing breeding stock for pig farming. I wanted to work close to the consumer in the food industry, but also remain close to pigs.

Most people don't grow up on farms or with livestock, and more and more of us are becoming detached from how food is produced and the interconnectivity between farming, the environment and how central food is to our own well-being. As a result our diets have become worse.

I am incredibly proud of the food we make at Cranswick and thankful to the British farmers who produce the animal feed and livestock that supply us. I am also passionate about the role of meat and poultry in our diets as essential sources of protein.

This book aims to change the narrative with regards to eating well and why we were in better shape when we prepared and consumed wholesome, natural, fresh and minimally processed foods.

These recipes celebrate our multi-cultural community at Cranswick. They're nutritionally balanced, high in protein and provide a good source of fibre *– a true omnivore's diet.*

Food has sustained human existence
explores how it shaped our cultures
sustainable eating

ınd health over centuries. This book
ınd how clues to healthier and more
exist in our past

HUMANS ARE OMNIVORES

Humans are omnivores: you can tell by our teeth. Our front teeth, incisors and canines are there for biting and tearing meat (like carnivores) and our molars are there for chewing vegetation (like herbivores).

Animals with both sets of teeth tend to be omnivores and this is a major part of how humankind has managed to populate all corners of the globe, as a resilient and dominant mammal, able to survive on whatever food source is available.

As we have become more domesticated as a species we have moved further away from our natural behaviours. The hunter, gatherer and farmer moved to the city, moved a lot less in their daily lives and over-consumed more abundant calories from often highly [ultra] processed foods.

Previous generations had to adapt to shortages of food; we now have an abundance of food, yet still fail to nourish ourselves adequately.

Our diets, despite the abundance and availability of a wide variety of food products, have become more and more dependent upon wheat (Europe) and corn (the Americas) due to their high yields and the huge number of calories they can convert per hectare, supporting increasing numbers of urban dwellers.

Many modern processed food products are derived from these key global crops, but in many cases they are highly refined, becoming far removed from the original natural product which contained more of the nutrients and fibre.

Animals have always been a key food source for mankind. Our nomadic forefathers travelled with goats and sheep, providing meat and dairy products. As we moved to more settled populations our domesticated species changed to pigs and chickens which would be fed on the same base commodities of wheat and corn that supported our species to thrive in ever increasing numbers.

These grains and the meat from pigs and chickens shaped our culture. They became central to how humans supported themselves and part of a food ecosystem that supported and regenerated itself and the land with mixed farming, livestock and plants, fertilising and maintaining the health of the soil.

Livestock farming in rotatio
of maintaining healthy and

with cereals is an essential part
fertile soils for the future

FARMING

Farming and the production of food has always been essential to developing communities and pivotal to how human settlements thrived. Pigs and chickens ate the same basic foods as us – cereals such as wheat and barley as well as our waste food – so they became our main 'domesticated' animals. They played an important role within a naturally regenerating food ecosystem. The land was used for mixed farming, with livestock and plants grown in synergy, fertilising the land whilst maintaining the health of the soils and wider natural environment.

Livestock is key to a sustainable agricultural system. Manure and natural bedding materials such as straw are vital in maintaining and improving the soil's ability to cycle nutrients to the next season's crops by increasing organic matter levels. This reduces the need for synthetic fertilisers and improves the soil structure and its water-holding capacity, thereby improving its resistance to drought.

Pig manure is rich in essential nutrients such as nitrogen, phosphorus and potassium, all of which are vital for plant growth. There is as much biodiversity within a healthy soil as there is above the surface and pig manure contains a wide variety of microorganisms that help maintain that natural balance and allow the soils to efficiently recycle and release nutrients for plant growth.

Cover crops of grass and legumes can accelerate the soil's ability to sequester carbon by increasing soil organic matter whilst also improving the soil's structure which in turn reduces soil erosion. Well-managed crop rotations, that utilise livestock within them, will maintain and build soil health. The end result is soils that can be one of the largest natural carbon sinks available to us. Lengthening field rotations to include livestock and a wide range of crops improves the resilience of our food system and the wider natural environment.

Pigs and chickens are highly efficient converters of grain to protein, making them very affordable meats, key to nourishing a growing global population. Their carbon emissions are amongst the lowest of the species we rear for meat. Pigs have been part of mixed farming for many years, turning cereals into a year-round source of protein as well as consuming waste and providing organic fertiliser for the land.

We believe that the clues to the future of sustainable farming lie in the past; a mixed agriculture system where crops are rotated on land where livestock manure naturally fertilises the soil, minimising the need for chemicals, respecting the land and animals that feed on it.

Pigs provide us with one of the
protein and pork is the mos

ichest sources of high-quality
onsumed meat in the world

Pigs

Pigs became a domesticated source of food around 7,000 to 10,000 years ago. Early humans in regions like the Near East and China began to capture and breed wild boars, which were abundant and relatively easy to manage. Pigs are like us – omnivorous – and can thrive on a varied diet, allowing them to be raised in diverse environments. They reproduce quickly, with a single sow able to produce multiple litters each year, ensuring a steady supply of meat. As agriculture developed, communities recognised the benefits of raising pigs alongside crops.

They could consume food scraps and leftovers, making them efficient converters of resources. Pork became popular due to its taste, culinary versatility and nutritional value. Over time, pigs spread across different cultures and regions, evolving into various breeds that cater to specific culinary traditions and farming practices.

The pig as a source of nutrition and primary protein transcends our cultural divides to such a degree that in China, the first symbol of a home was a pig in a house, representing how they were used to consume a family's waste and provide a source of energy and protein throughout the winter.

Similarly, in Japan, one of the most coveted gifts you could give would be a square of belly pork in a wooden box, specifically in the Oshōgatsu (New Year) season. Pigs are associated with abundance and wealth and giving pork as a gift is believed to bring prosperity in the coming year.

In Western Europe, German culture is synonymous with the sausage in many forms; the Germans eat more sausages per capita than any other nation in the world. The Schweinfest is a cultural celebration in some regions and the sausage features heavily on menus during Oktoberfest.

Pigs hold significant cultural importance in various societies around the world, symbolising a range of concepts from prosperity to fertility:

Fertility and abundance – In many cultures, pigs are associated with fertility and abundance. For instance, in some African traditions, pigs are seen as symbols of wealth and prosperity due to their reproductive capabilities.

Culinary traditions – Pork is an ideal meat to make dry-cured meats such as chorizo, pancetta, prosciutto and salami. In countries like Spain, they are celebrated in dishes like Jamón Ibérico, often referred to as 'the olive oil pork', a meat which supports 'good' cholesterol and lowers bad. Some of the finest pork products in world come from the Emilia Romagna region of northern Italy, where they produce the Gran Suina Padane, the heavy Italian pigs used to produce the king of hams (and the ham of kings!), Prosciutto di Parma. Pork also became a staple in America's BBQ culture in the 18th century because pigs were a cost-effective, low-maintenance source of food.

Folklore and mythology – Pigs appear in various myths and folktales. In Norse mythology, the boar Gullinbursti is a symbol of fertility and abundance, while in some cultures, pigs represent the cycle of life and death.

Social status and wealth – In some societies, owning pigs can signify social status and wealth. For example, in parts of South East Asia, pigs are often given as gifts during important ceremonies.

Festivals and celebrations – Many cultures have festivals centred around pigs, such as the Chinese New Year, where the pig is one of the zodiac animals symbolising wealth and good fortune. The Hawaiian luau is a traditional feast where the kalua pig is the centrepiece.

Chickens are great value for money
will soon overtake pork as the

and a versatile source of protein that
world's most consumed meat

Chickens

Chickens were domesticated from wild ancestors, primarily the red junglefowl, around 8,000 years ago in South East Asia. Over time, humans began to appreciate them as a food source due to their relatively quick growth and ability to lay eggs consistently.

The domestication process involved selective breeding for traits such as docility, size and egg production. Chickens proved adaptable to various environments, which contributed to their spread across the globe. Chickens were already a common source of meat and eggs by the time of the Roman Empire and their popularity continued to grow, leading to the poultry farming we see today.

The broiler chicken, farmed for meat, became prevalent after World War II as food security came up the agenda as we exited rationing. It was Lord Sainsbury who pioneered a lot of the development of the poultry industry we have today with a view to making it more widely available and affordable for many people.

Chicken is due to overtake pork as the most consumed protein in the world due to its affordability, versatility and global cultural acceptance – it's less likely to be restricted by religious and cultural beliefs.

For every human being on the planet, there are three chickens: the earth is home to some 25 billion chickens from the jungles of Malaysia to the small-holdings and allotments of the western world.

Chickens are associated with good luck and fortune in Chinese culture in the same way as the pig. Chickens and roosters are also a well-known feature in Chinese New Year traditions.

In western cultures on the other hand the chicken is associated with simplicity, rural life and farm traditions. The rooster is the symbol of France and the prestigious Poulet de Bresse is famed for its flavour and texture and boasts protected designation of origin or appellation d'origine contrôlée (AOC) status. They also feature strongly in many other cultures, highlighting their importance as a world food.

Chickens hold various cultural significances across different societies, reflecting their roles in agriculture, religion and everyday life:

Fertility and prosperity – In many cultures, chickens symbolise fertility, abundance and prosperity. Their ability to lay eggs consistently makes them a representation of new life. In Mexico chickens often feature in art including Talavera pottery as symbols of luck and protection.

Culinary importance – Chickens are integral to numerous culinary traditions worldwide. Dishes featuring chicken are staples in many cuisines, from fried chicken in the United States to coq au vin in France, highlighting their versatility and central role in family meals.

Religious and spiritual significance – In some cultures, chickens are used in rituals and offerings. Some African and Haitian voodoo traditions use chickens in religious rituals as offerings to spirits and deities. In Balinese cultures chickens are considered sacred and are used in various ceremonies and rituals often associated with purification and protection.

Folklore and mythology – Chickens often appear in folklore and stories, often symbolising caution or timidity (the 'chicken-hearted' character).

Festivals and celebrations – Chickens play a role in various festivals and celebrations. In some Asian cultures, specific dishes involving chicken are prepared during New Year celebrations to bring good luck.

Cultural practices and customs – In many rural communities, chickens are kept for eggs and meat, serving as a source of sustenance. They are also often featured in local traditions, such as cock-fighting, which is still a cultural practice in some countries.

The Mediterranean diet, rich in
is considered one of the

oils, vegetables, meat and dairy,
healthiest in the world

Mediterranean cuisine

Cultivation

Olives – Cultivated for centuries in Greece, Italy and Spain and now enjoyed worldwide. Known for their healthy oils, olives are associated with 'blue zone' areas which have high life expectancy and are often also locations where, culturally, there is more cooking from scratch, far less reliance on ultra-processed foods and a closeness to agriculture.

The Kalamata olive is one of the most revered, a large, dark purple olive with a smooth, meaty texture, named after the city of Kalamata in Greece. Often used as table olives, they're usually preserved in wine vinegar or olive oil. Kalamata olives, which cannot be harvested green, must be hand-picked to avoid bruising.

The Italian Nocellara olive is a large green olive, with a mild, buttery flavour. It's grown to produce extra virgin olive oil and for eating: it's the ideal olive to serve with antipasti.

Olive Oil – Extra virgin olive oil is one of the healthiest fats, with high levels of antioxidants and anti-inflammatory properties. It makes a great dressing and can be used for cooking but has a low smoke point so only over a medium heat.

Chickpeas – Houmous is associated with Greek and Mediterranean foods but its origins are in the Middle East, where chickpeas form a central part of the diet and cuisine. In Israel, Palestine and Lebanon, houmous is a staple food and eaten almost every day, not as dip but as a main meal. Traditional houmous has a smoother texture than much of that produced in the UK. However, the key ingredients remain the same: chickpeas, tahini, olive oil, lemon juice, garlic and salt, making it a source of fibre, protein and healthy fat.

Meat and dairy

Greece and Cyprus – Feta cheese, made primarily from sheep's and goats' milk is a great accompaniment for olives, particularly the kalamata.

Halloumi, the Greek grilling cheese, originates in Cyprus and is made from sheep's and goats' milk. The protein and fat in halloumi can slow the emptying of your stomach, which may help stabilise your blood sugar levels after meals.

Spain – The wide variety of geography and climate across Spain creates diversity of agriculture resulting in more than 150 different types of cheese being produced across the country.

The far north of the country has rich pastureland best suited to dairy herds where cheeses such as Cabrales, an artisanal blue cheese, is produced from cow's and goats' milk. To the west, the more mountainous region of Extremadura produces cheeses such as Viejo Maestro, a semi-firm, mild and creamy goats' cheese.

Finally, over to La Mancha, just south of the capital Madrid, where a colder, drier climate at altitude lends itself to sheep and goat farming creating iconic Spanish cheeses such as Ibérico Riserva, a hard cheese that has an exceptional flavour with nutty and slightly spicy notes.

Spanish cured meats are also a product of the country's history, culture and terrain, most notably the Jamón Serrano or 'ham from the mountains' where it is traditionally cured due to the cooler temperatures and humidity. It is similar to Italian prosciutto but with a dryer texture, deeper colour and stronger flavour, due to stronger salting and a longer curing phase of up to 18 months.

Jamón Ibérico steals the show as Spain's most revered ham. It's produced from the unique Iberian pig which exists in a symbiotic relationship within the Dehesa, the great oak forest of western Spain and Portugal. These pigs roam free during la montenera, or fattening period (from the end of October to the end of February), often doubling their weight as they gorge on acorns, which give an intense flavour to this heavily marbled pork.

Chorizo is a cured pork sausage originating from the Iberian Peninsula and produced in both Spain and Portugal. It's produced both as a fresh sausage for cooking, boiling and barbecuing, as well as a fully fermented and ready-to-eat tapas product.

Other notable Spanish specialties are lomo and salchichón, which are cured and air-dried in a similar way. Lomo is a lean, cured meat, served in slices and made by marinating and air-drying a pork tenderloin. Salchichón is another cured sausage, without the pimentón seasoning of chorizo, but flavoured with black peppercorns.

Charcuterie is also produced in France, with notable specialties such as jambon de Bayonne and saucisson sec. The Alto Adige and South Tyrolean regions of Northern Italy which border Switzerland, Germany and France produce favourites such as prosciutto di speck, whilst Germany is celebrated for its Black Forest ham, Bavarian ham, bierwurst and bratwurst, along with a diverse array of regional specialty sausages and salamis.

Italy – The foods of Emilia Romagna and the wider Pianura Padane demonstrate the synergy between animals and nature. Most famously the Parma ham and the lesser known culatello (where Parma is the king, culatello is queen) exist because of the fertility of the Po River flood plain, the climate of warm summers and cold winters with brisk salty breezes sweeping in from the Ligurian sea and the availability of high-quality salt which was used to cure the meat.

The Gran Suina Padane, or Italian heavy pigs of the Po Valley in Emilia Romagna, are grown predominantly for their hams. Parma is exported all over the world. It holds the Denominazione d'Origine Protetta (DOP) mark, which translates as Protected Designation of Origin meaning it can only be produced around the Parma region. One of the many reasons this ham is so special is because it uses pork from heavier, older animals, fed a diet which includes whey, the bi-product of Parmigiano Reggiano and Grana Padano cheese production.

Parmigiano Reggiano is the principal hard cheese of Emillia Romagna – it goes brilliantly on the plate with Parma ham and extra virgin olive oil.

The most famous Italian salami is probably the Milano salami, but the king of salamis is perhaps the Felino, again from the Parma region and often sliced diagonally and slightly thicker than the Milano.

THE FOODS OF EMILIA ROMAGNA AND THE WIDER PIANURA PADANE DEMONSTRATE THE SYNERGY BETWEEN ANIMALS AND NATURE

JUST EAT PROPER FOOD

The current healthy eating messages should be revised. We'd like to see them focused more on an inclusive diet: one which promotes the foods that nourish us, rather than cancelling entire food groups, such as dairy, gluten or meat.

Instead we should be prioritising the benefits of eating different foods that balance nutrients. We believe 'eat more vegetables' is a much a more useful message than 'eat less meat'.

Pork and chicken are wholefoods and even processed pork products do not have to be ultra-processed. By their very nature they engender a back-to-basics approach, simple cooking and preparation, using store cupboard ingredients; scratch cooking which in turn will make it easier to get your key nutrients in balance without over-consuming the empty calories present in ultra-convenient foods and ready meals.

We've been bombarded with misleading messages about healthy eating, often promoting quick fixes. Eat less fat. Eat low fat. Eat as few calories as possible, consume less salt, eat less sugar (although that one probably is a good idea!).

Rather than just cutting calories, focus on the protein content of each meal as well as including a variety of vegetables, salad and grains. Eating lean pork and chicken is great place to start, but other cuts and products such as belly pork and sausages can also be a great source of protein.

We passionately believe in eating well for health. Healthy eating should be part of a balanced lifestyle, not something done a few weeks each year. It should be enjoyable and sustainable, without over-restricting calories or food groups; otherwise, you'll never stick to it. It should also be realistic: it doesn't matter if one day you eat some chocolate or have a dessert if you balance your food intake and compensate for it in the following days.

Portion size and variety play a vital role in our general health too: a healthy, balanced diet is crucial for overall well-being and plays a key role in preventing chronic diseases. The foundation of such a diet lies in natural, whole and minimally processed foods. Meat, dairy, fish and eggs provide essential proteins, while animal fats and carbohydrates offer vital energy. Vegetables are our primary source of fibre, vitamins and micronutrients.

Lots of people fall short of both their protein needs and the recommended 'five a day' guideline for fruit and vegetables and overindulge in sugar and carbohydrates. If you eat a wide variety of fresh meat and vegetables, you won't need to rely on vitamin and mineral supplements. A nutrient-dense natural diet provides the body with all the vitamins and minerals it needs.

Our recipes have been created to achieve balance: fifty dishes that not only taste great, but also fit into a healthy, nutritionally complete, varied and sustainable diet, providing roughly the recommended amounts of nutrients per meal.

They include new takes on traditional classics from across the globe, and recipes that reflect the latest trends inspired by the diverse international cultures of our teams.

'Eat more veg' is far more

constructive than 'eat less meat'

PRIORITISE PROTEIN

EAT MORE VEG

BALANCE CALORIES

Principles for a healthy diet

These 3 simple messages underpin a healthy diet, providing everything you need to completely nourish the body and promote long-term well-being.

Prioritise protein – Eating more protein, **30g-60g per meal**, keeps you full and satisfied. Under-eat protein and it's all too easy to overeat cheap carbohydrates and over-consume empty calories.

Eat more veg – Vegetables have few calories and not much protein (macronutrients), but they are a major source of essential fibre, micronutrients and vitamins. Eat as many different varieties as you can! Most people don't eat enough fibre – we should be aiming for **30g per day**.

Balance calories – Fat isn't the enemy! It's increasingly recognised that healthy fats are a good source of energy and essential for health. Balancing your meals and keeping an eye on portion size is all-important. An average male should consume **2,500kcal per day** and a female **2,000kcal per day**. This isn't about consuming as few calories as possible: you need energy for your body's essential functions. Too much of a calorie deficit and you'll find yourself reaching for the biscuit tin! Simply put, if you don't want to gain weight, don't consume more energy than you expend.

THERE ARE FIVE ESSENTIAL NUTRIENTS FOUND IN FOOD THAT THE BODY USES TO PERFORM BASIC FUNCTIONS, STAY HEALTHY AND GROW

Macronutrients

Protein – Proteins are macronutrients in food that help build the body as it grows. Animal sources like meat, eggs and milk are generally better sources of protein than plants.

Fats and lipids – A broad term for fats, oils and other fatty compounds found in food. A source of energy needed for activity, growth and bodily functions like breathing, digesting food and keeping warm.

Carbohydrates – A source of energy, classed as either simple or complex. Simple carbohydrates, like sugar, are broken down quickly for energy, while complex carbohydrates, like fibre and starch, are broken down more slowly for sustained energy.

Micronutrients

Vitamins – Organic compounds that people need in small quantities. Each has a different role in maintaining health and bodily function.

Minerals – Can be macrominerals or microminerals, such as electrolytes that help cells turn nutrients into energy when dissolved in water.

Protein

Protein is a vital part of a healthy diet. It's a macronutrient that breaks down into amino acids which help the body to grow and repair. It's a key component of bones, muscles, skin, hair and nails, which is used to carry oxygen throughout the human body.

Enzymes created from protein help digest food and create new cells and chemicals. It plays a role in hormone regulation and also helps maintain the normal pH of bodily fluids and a protein-rich diet helps lower blood pressure. It has a higher thermic effect than fat or carbs, which means protein can increase the number of calories you burn and reduce food cravings.

The amount of protein recommended depends on age, gender, weight and health and a high protein diet can even help slow down muscle loss. As a rule of thumb, you need 1g protein per day per pound of body weight or 2.2g protein per kilogram.

Most of us will fall short of this target. Prioritising protein at breakfast is a good start; all too often we start the day with a cereal or carbohydrate-based meal or, even worse, a sugary cereal or pastry!

White meat and eggs are both primary sources of protein. Both pork and chicken have multiple nutritional benefits; both are lean meats, low in calories and with strong and varied nutritional profiles.

Pork and chicken make up a large portion of the protein content of our recipes, accompanied by a variety of vegetables, salad and grains. Lean pork and chicken are great places to start when adopting a healthier lifestyle but other cuts and products, such as belly pork and sausages, still have their place in a varied and nutritionally balanced diet over time.

MEAT, FISH, POULTRY AND EGGS ARE THE BEST PRIMARY SOURCES OF PROTEIN

The table below highlights the protein you get from pork and chicken (cooked) per 100g. Pork and chicken have the highest % protein and come just below prawns and cod in terms of the protein content per calorie consumed.

Per 100g cooked	*Protein (%)*	*Protein (g)*	*Calories (kcal)*	*Calories /g Protein*
Prawns	23.5	23.5	102	4.34
Cod	24.6	24.6	106	4.31
Chicken	31.9	31.9	147	4.61
Pork loin	31.6	31.6	184	5.82
Beef sirloin	26.6	26.6	176	6.62
Salmon	24.6	24.6	239	9.72
Chickpeas	8.4	8.4	142	16.9

Fat does not make you fat; it's a
key functions like breathing

key source of energy, maintaining
digesting food and keeping warm

Fats and lipids

Fat is essential for our bodies. We would aim for around 30% of our consumed calories coming from healthy fats, including animal and dairy products. This energy source just needs to be balanced with your overall calorie intake.

Rich source of energy – Animal fats are calorie-dense, providing a concentrated source of energy.

Essential fatty acids – Certain animal fats contain essential fatty acids like omega-3 fatty acids, which are important for brain function, reducing inflammation and maintaining heart health.

Absorption of fat-soluble vitamins – Animal fats help in the absorption of fat-soluble vitamins (A, D, E and K).

Contains conjugated linoleic acid (CLA) – Found in the fat of grass-fed animals, it has been linked to improved fat metabolism and immune support.

(Good) cholesterol for hormone production – Cholesterol in animal fats is a precursor to producing essential hormones like oestrogen, testosterone and cortisol. It is also vital for maintaining healthy cell membranes.

Supports brain health – Animal fats are crucial for brain structure and function and are necessary for proper nerve signalling.

Satiating – Fats slow digestion and promote a feeling of fullness, helping to regulate appetite and prevent overeating. Consuming adequate fats can aid in maintaining a healthy weight.

Minimal processing – Natural animal fats are minimally processed compared to industrial seed oils, reducing the risk of consuming harmful trans fats or oxidised oils.

Carbohydrates

Carbohydrates mainly provide us with a source of energy (calories). The number of calories you need per day depends on your age, height, sex, weight, activity level and metabolic health. To achieve a balanced diet you should aim to consume the right number of calories and balance carbs, protein, fat, fibre, vitamins and minerals. Managing calories effectively involves tracking your intake and understanding your energy needs. Eat more fruits and vegetables as they are high in fibre and nutrients. Balance and moderation are important too – the occasional treat will help you to maintain a sustainable approach to eating without feeling deprived.

Fibre is the indigestible part of plants that helps keep your digestive system healthy. It's essential for humans to function.

Fibre is found in fruits, vegetables, beans, lentils and starchy carbohydrates. It plays an important role in our diet. High-fibre foods can add bulk and texture, making food more satisfying to eat; they can promote a feeling of fullness which helps control appetite and reduce calorie intake, they can also help the digestive system. Fibre slows down the absorption of nutrients, leading to more stable blood sugar levels.

Certain fibres act as prebiotics, providing food for beneficial gut bacteria which can improve gut health. Overall, fibre contributes to both the nutritional quality and the physical properties of food, making it a crucial component of a healthy diet.

White meat doesn't contain any dietary fibre, so both pork and chicken should be paired with fibre-rich ingredients to achieve recommended daily fibre intake.

Salt is not the enemy; it's essentia
to properly hydrate the body anc
it if you're eating

:o your diet, balancing electrolytes
/ou're unlikely to over consume
natural wholefoods

Micronutrients

Vitamins

Vitamins are essential organic compounds, primarily obtained from food, that are crucial for the normal functioning of cells in the body. While humans can synthesise certain vitamins, such as vitamin D through skin exposure to sunlight, most of our vitamin intake comes from the foods we consume. Although vitamin supplements can be beneficial in certain situations, it is widely recognised that a balanced and varied diet provides all the vitamins the body needs for optimal health.

Minerals

Minerals like calcium, iron and zinc are absorbed by plants and animals from the environment and subsequently become part of the foods we eat. Like vitamins, these minerals are essential for maintaining optimal health. While they are available in supplement form, a well-balanced and varied diet can provide all the minerals the body needs.

Salt – Sodium is an extremely important electrolyte and an essential ion in extracellular fluid. It plays a pivotal role in enzyme operation and muscle contraction. It is important for balancing electrolytes and properly hydrating the body.

Maintains fluid balance – Sodium is essential for regulating the balance of fluids inside and outside cells.

Promotes nerve function – Sodium is key for transmitting electrical signals in the nervous system, enabling communication between the brain and body.

Aids muscle contraction – Sodium is required for muscle contraction, which includes the functioning of the heart and skeletal muscles.

Regulates blood pressure – While excessive sodium can lead to high blood pressure, maintaining the right balance supports normal blood pressure levels.

Recommended daily intake (RDI) – The general sodium recommendation is **2,300–2,400mg per day** (about one teaspoon of salt). Athletes or those in hot climates may require higher sodium intake due to loss through sweat.

As with everything, it's all about balance: our bodies need salt to function, but it's important to get it right. Too much sodium may lead to high blood pressure, kidney strain and an increased risk of heart disease and stroke, but too little can cause symptoms such as fatigue and confusion. Potassium helps counterbalance sodium, reducing the risk of high blood pressure. Bananas, oranges and leafy greens are great sources of potassium.

Opt for quality sources – Natural salts, like sea salt or Himalayan pink salt, can provide trace minerals, but their sodium content is similar to regular table salt.

Pork and chicken give us not only

minerals and micronutrients

protein, but also the key vitamins,
not readily found in plants

Pork ingredients

Vitamin B1 – Has an essential role in bodily functions and keeps your nervous system healthy.

Vitamin B2 – Helps with energy production in your body.

Vitamin B3 – Helps you to use sugars and fatty acids more efficiently. It produces energy in all body cells, aids function in the body such as growth and metabolism and is part of the normal functioning of the body's enzymes.

Vitamin B5 – Supports blood cell production and the conversion of the food you eat to energy.

Vitamin B6 – Supports the production of amino acids as well as contributing to producing vital chemicals including antibodies, haemoglobin and insulin.

Vitamin B12 – Aids blood formation and brain function.

Vitamin D – Increases the amount of calcium and phosphorus your body absorbs from food.

Vitamin E – Important for vision, reproduction and the health of blood, brain and skin. Strengthens the body's natural defence against illness and infection and is an antioxidant.

Collagen – Provides structure, support and strength to your skin, muscles, bones and connective tissues.

Iron – Prevents anaemia by aiding haemoglobin production. Helps metabolise protein. Provides support for the immune system, skin nourishment and improves sleep quality and reduces fatigue.

Magnesium – Supports energy production, muscle and nerve function, blood pressure regulation and heart rhythm.

Potassium – For general health; supports the kidneys, heart and other organs.

Phosphorus – For growth and maintenance.

Selenium – An essential mineral which helps prevent cancer, heart, autoimmune and thyroid disease.

Zinc – For a healthy brain and immune system.

✓high protein ✓vitamin rich ✓mineral rich

Nutritional information

Typical values per 150g uncooked pork loin steak

Protein	29g
Energy	311kcal
Fat	21.8g

Minerals

Potassium	495mg
Phosphorus	286.5mg
Magnesium	31.5mg
Zinc	2mg
Iron	0.9mg
Selenium	16.5mcg/dl

Vitamins

Vitamin B3 (Niacin)	8.4mg
Vitamin B5 (Pantothenic acid)	1.6mg
Vitamin B1 (Thiamin)	1.4mg
Vitamin B6 (Pyridoxine)	1.1mg
Vitamin B2 (Riboflavin)	0.3mg
Vitamin E	0.1mg
Vitamin B12 (Cobalamin)	1.5mcg/dl

Chicken ingredients

Vitamin A – Supports the immune system to protect against illness and infection, keeps your skin healthy and supports your vision.

Vitamin B1 – Has an essential role in bodily functions and keeps your nervous system healthy.

Vitamin B2 – Helps with energy production in your body.

Vitamin B3 – Helps you to use sugars and fatty acids more efficiently. It produces energy in all body cells, aids function in the body such as growth and metabolism and is part of the normal functioning of the body's enzymes.

Vitamin B5 – Supports blood cell production and the conversion of the food you eat to energy.

Vitamin B6 – Supports the production of amino acids as well as contributing to producing vital chemicals including antibodies, haemoglobin and insulin.

Vitamin B9 – Supports the body to produce red blood cells.

Vitamin B12 – Aids blood formation and brain function.

Vitamin C – Helps to protect cells and keep them healthy, maintaining skin, blood vessels, bones and cartilage, and promotes wound healing.

Vitamin D – Increases the amount of calcium and phosphorus your body absorbs from food.

Vitamin E – Important for vision, reproduction and the health of blood, brain and skin. Strengthens the body's natural defence against illness and infection and is an antioxidant.

Vitamin K – Helps wounds heal properly.

Collagen – Provides structure, support and strength to your skin, muscles, bones and connective tissues.

Iron – Prevents anaemia by aiding haemoglobin production. Helps metabolise protein. Provides support for the immune system, skin nourishment and improves sleep quality and reduces fatigue.

Magnesium – Supports energy production, muscle and nerve function, blood pressure regulation and heart rhythm.

Potassium – For general health; supports the kidneys, heart and other organs.

Phosphorus – For growth and maintenance.

Selenium – An essential mineral which helps prevent cancer, heart, autoimmune and thyroid disease.

Zinc – For a healthy brain and immune system.

✓high protein ✓vitamin rich ✓mineral rich

Nutritional information

Typical values per 150g uncooked chicken breast

Protein	36g
Energy	159kcal
Fat	1.7g

Minerals

Potassium	555mg
Phosphorus	330mg
Magnesium	44mg
Zinc	1.1mg
Iron	0.8mg
Selenium	18mcg/dl

Vitamins

Vitamin B3 (Niacin)	16.1mg
Vitamin B5 (Pantothenic acid)	1.9mg
Vitamin B6 (Pyridoxine)	0.8mg
Vitamin B1 (Thiamin)	0.2mg
Vitamin B2 (Riboflavin)	0.2mg
Vitamin E	0.2mg
Vitamin D	0.3mcg/dl

Cooking with pork

Provenance and breeding play a vital role in texture and flavour. The key to using the right cut is to remember that if you want a dish that is light and quick to prepare, then look for a cut that is lean with little fat. A stir-fry, for instance, needs a cut like pork loin or tenderloin that will cook quickly and can be cut into smaller pieces. But fat is essential to certain recipes. If you're going for roast pork with crackling then you need a crackling boneless loin joint, which has extra fat to deliver the 'crackle' and protect the meat during the longer cooking time. Pork belly and shoulder also need to be cooked slowly, their fat content keeping them moist and succulent.

The breeds of pigs we rear are selected with eating quality in mind. Our Hampshire pork is selected to deliver a tender, white, lean meat, grown outdoors to RSPCA high welfare standards and finished in deep straw-bedded barns. We also use a Duroc or Jersey Red pig, originating from Jersey USA in the early 1900s, which are certified heritage breeds that deliver increased intramuscular fat for more tasty, succulent pork.

Rib roast – The king of pork joints! This cut carries a little fat at the shoulder end, which helps keep it succulent and tender. It's served either rind-on or rindless. Leave it rind-on for perfect crackling and score it for a stunning roast. The important thing to remember is to be careful not to overcook it – use a meat thermometer and you can't go wrong! You need to deeply score the rind through the fat, but not into the meat. Then pour freshly boiled water over the top to open the scoring. Dry the pork and then rub it with olive oil and sprinkle with lots of salt. Roast it in the oven for 45 minutes at 230°C – this allows the crackling to pop and achieve a golden bubbly crust. Then turn the oven down until the core temperature reaches 68°C. Finally rest the meat for 15 minutes to allow it to relax before slicing and serving.

Crackling boneless loin joint – Crackling is one of the most loved parts of pork, yet people tell me they can't get the rind to crackle. You simply need to start with the right meat – you need at least 14mm of fat cover, deeply scored. Take a whole boneless pork joint and carefully score it in rows ½cm apart, to enable easy slicing and portioning once cooked, being careful to cut all the way through the rind but not into the fat. It's then cooked in the same way as the rib roast above.

Pork chops – Cut between the ribs and with the chine bone removed. A pork chop is traditionally cut between the ribs for a super thick and succulent chop. We've taken this one step further and left the rib bone in and then French-trimmed the bone to create a pork tomahawk chop. This can be cooked in lots of ways, but suits a very hot and fast griddle pan or BBQ best to sear the outside of the meat leaving it succulent and tender in the middle.

Pork loin – A cut from the pig's back, between the ribs and back fat, that's tender and full of flavour. Typically this is a lean cut of pork, hot and fast cooking is best, quickly pan-fried on a high heat to avoid over cooking.

Boston butt – This cut originated in America. It's from the upper shoulder with the shoulder blade running through it. When slow cooked the bone conducts heat evenly through the joint and breaks down the collagen to create a great tasting, succulent piece of pork. Classically cooked on the BBQ/smoker very low and slow, a 5kg Boston butt will take around 12 hours to perfectly cook.

Neck fillet – Great for pulled pork because of its marbled meat. The chine side is the prime shoulder cut for roasting and is also good strung and tied as a joint. Long slow cooking lets the fat render down and the meat tenderise, resulting in a lovely juicy piece of pork that is full of flavour. The rind can be left on the neck fillet for excellent crackling.

Pork belly – Pork belly needs to be cooked slowly allowing the fat to render down, the meat to become super tender and the fat or rind to crisp up. Exceptional in the air fryer if you want that crispy crackling.

Gammon joint – The traditional Sunday roast joint – with a good amount of fat it will crackle beautifully. It must be deeply scored through the rind and into the fat, but not the meat. The leg is also cured to make gammon. Take care not to overcook your gammon joint as they are typically lean cuts of pork, once your core temperature of 68°C is reached, let the joint rest, this will ensure juicy and succulent meat.

Tenderloin fillet – An underrated cut of pork, super-lean and perfect for hot and fast cooking like pork loin. Tenderloin is really easy cooking and great for really healthy dishes.

Cooking with chicken

We all remember chicken that really tasted of chicken. Our chickens are reared on our own farms in and around Norfolk, where the chickens hatch from their eggs naturally in the barns which enhances the welfare of the chickens and contributes to the meat quality. Food miles are key to preserving sustainable food production and the environment.

There are two main types of chicken. The first is free range, these slower-growing birds from specific breeds are reared outdoors during the day and protected indoors at night. The longer the chicken develops, the more the flavour intensifies. However, it also means that muscle fibres are more developed which gives the meat a firmer texture. This is an important consideration when it comes to cooking.

The second type of bird is a high-welfare Red Tractor breed, which is raised indoors and achieves a desired weight faster. This process produces birds that are more delicate and tender, which many consumers prefer. This type of chicken is also much cheaper – sometimes as much as half the price of a free-range bird.

With pork, the secret lies in the amount of fat in each cut, but chicken is naturally not as fatty. Remove the skin and the meat is almost uniformly lean. Like pork this can be an advantage in quick cooking. However, for slow cooking, such as a roast, the fat plays an important part. What you really need to take care with is the moisture content. Keeping the skin on to protect the chicken whilst cooking helps to keep the moisture in and produces succulent meat.

French housewives have an expression that goes 'always choose a mad chicken'. What they mean is that the best-flavoured meat comes from a bird that has worked its legs by running around a lot. In the UK we consume chicken primarily for the breast meat, but we should do a better job of consuming all parts of the bird. The breast meat is very white and lean which the consumer loves but the dark meat has more flavour. The most flavoursome part of a chicken is the leg: the thighs and drumsticks are great cuts for stews and curries as they're so succulent. The breast is leaner and needs more attention so it doesn't dry out.

Cooking quickly or keeping the skin on when cooking helps to keep the moisture in (and the skin is delicious when crisp). The recipes we've included in this book take advantage of each cut's unique characteristics and celebrate their different flavours.

Whole chicken – As with all meat, you need to buy the best you can: look out for free-range or British Red Tractor chicken. Don't be scared to have a go at butchering a whole chicken: it's easy and takes no time at all. It can be quickly cut into breasts, thighs, drumsticks and wings. Roasting a chicken is so simple, a 1.5kg chicken will roast in 1 hour 20 minutes at 180°C . Don't be scared to have a go at butchering a whole chicken, either before or after its cooked. Cutting the bird into its key cuts makes it so much easier to get those juicy dark meats.

Chicken breast – Widely used, a cut from the underside of the chicken, that's tender and has a mild flavour. Chicken breast is the leanest part of the chicken so be careful not to overcook as it will dry out easily. It can be cooked in so many ways; pan frying or on the BBQ over hot coals are my favourites. Chicken breast is really versatile and lends itself to quick cooking either as a whole piece or cut into strips and chunks for pan-frying.

Thigh fillet – A superbly flavoursome piece of meat which works well for many recipes in this book. Thighs are very popular in Asian cooking – and taste amazing! Leg meat on chicken is now almost as white as the breast, but it still delivers much more flavour. Thigh meat would be my cut of choice because, like breast, it can be cooked in every possible way achieving different flavours and textures.

Legs and drumsticks – Wonderfully tasty pieces of meat. Whole legs are ideal for jerk chicken and cooking on the bone develops the flavour and tenderness of the meat. Legs and drumsticks are best cooked in the oven or BBQ to allow slower cooking to cook through to the bone and render down the natural fat in the legs.

Wings – A classic of American cuisine, 1.3 billion wings are consumed on Super Bowl weekend alone! There are two key cuts, the mids and primes. Chicken wings are best cooked in the oven, BBQ or air fryer on a high heat to crisp up the really tasty skin.

HOG &
BEYOND
Snapback

"Developing the following recipes has been a rewarding challenge. As chefs, we naturally gravitate toward creating incredible tasting food, even when it's not always kind to our waistlines! Keeping health and balanced nutrition at the forefront pushed us to think more creatively about portion sizes, ingredient choices and the diverse array of produce available. The result – delicious dishes that satisfy both the palate and our nutritional needs"

Simon Woods

The following recipes have been produced as authentically as possible using techniques adapted to deliver nutritionally balanced takes on global food

BRITISH

There are some great ***British*** recipe
course, around the food we produc
have in season. Traditional British foo
The classic roast is filled with protei
form of meat, potatoes and vegetable
and East Anglia, where traditionall
peas, beans and potatoes, henc

arming, hearty dishes centred, of
the British Isles and the produce we
rovides a good balance of nutrients.
arbohydrates and micronutrients in the
Ve produce a lot of pork in Yorkshire
rain was produced in rotation with
ne tradition for meat and two veg

This lighter version of the traditional Sunday roast is ideal for spring and summer. Fantastic crackling is the ultimate goal with roast pork. We've used an air fryer to create unbeatable, foolproof crackling and succulent, tender pork in half the normal time. The sautéed garden pea medley contains eight different vegetables, so it really delivers on fibre.

AIR FRYER BONELESS PORK LOIN CRACKLING JOINT, MINTED NEW POTATOES AND SAUTÉED GARDEN PEA MEDLEY

Nutritional information

Amount per serving	
Protein	45.8g
Fat	56.4g
Carbohydrates	52.0g
Fibre	11.6g
Energy	878kcal

Serves: 6
Prep time: 30 minutes
Cooking time: 80 minutes

for the pork loin
1.2 kg rind-on boneless pork loin joint, *straight scored*
table salt
20ml sunflower oil

for the new potatoes
800g new potatoes
50g salted butter
10g fresh mint, chopped
sea salt and cracked black pepper

for the garden pea medley
300g frozen garden peas
1 tbsp sunflower oil
3 large carrots, *peeled, halved and thinly sliced*
300g stem broccoli
1 red pepper, *finely diced*
1 yellow pepper, *finely diced*
1 large red onion, *peeled and finely diced*
1 large leek, *washed and sliced*
2 cloves garlic, *peeled and minced*
5g salted butter
10g flat leaf parsley, leaves only, *roughly chopped*

to serve
50g honey
50g wholegrain mustard
30g meat juice from the air fryer

For the pork loin, remove the pork from the fridge 30 minutes prior to cooking, place onto a tray and liberally rub table salt into the rind. Leave to sit for 30 minutes. Preheat the air fryer to 180°C, scrape off the salt and dry the rind with a paper towel. Brush with oil, place into the air fryer and cook for 60-80 minutes. Use a meat thermometer to check you have a core temperature of 68°C, remove from the air fryer, cover with foil and rest for 10 minutes – this should bring the core temperature up to 72°C.

For the new potatoes, slice the potatoes in half and cover with cold water in a large saucepan. Bring to a rolling boil and cook for 8-10 minutes or until you can easily pierce the centre of the potato with the tip of a knife. Drain the potatoes and whilst still hot add the butter and fresh mint. Once the butter has melted stir the potatoes gently to fully cover in the butter mixture and season with salt and black pepper.

For the garden pea medley, defrost the peas in warm water and put to one side. Add the oil to a frying pan over a medium heat. Add the carrots and sauté on a low heat until softened, then add the broccoli and cook for a further 5 minutes. Add the peppers, red onion, leek and garlic and cook gently until softened and starting to brown, then add the peas and cook on a high heat for 2 minutes. Finally add the butter and chopped parsley and check the seasoning.

To serve, mix the honey and mustard together in a small saucepan over a medium heat, add the meat juices and bring to the boil, then turn off the heat. Slice the pork and place onto a plate, serve the peas and potatoes alongside, and pour the honey mustard sauce over the pork.

We couldn't do a chapter on British recipes without including a full English! This recipe makes this delicious and traditional treat easier, healthier and quicker to clean up afterwards, as everything except the eggs and spinach goes into the air fryer.

AIR FRYER FULL ENGLISH BREAKFAST

Nutritional information

Amount per serving	
Protein	53.7g
Fat	54.6g
Carbohydrates	48.2g
Fibre	6.7g
Energy	914kcal

Serves: 2
Prep time: 10 minutes
Cooking time: 20 minutes

for the breakfast
2 premium pork sausages
100g baby button mushrooms
1 tsp extra virgin olive oil
4 rashers dry-cured air-dried smoked back bacon
80g cherry tomatoes on the vine
sea salt and cracked black pepper

for the spinach
200g baby spinach
10g salted butter
sea salt and cracked black pepper

to finish
2 large free-range eggs
2 slices wholemeal and rye toast
20g salted butter
5g fresh parsley

For the breakfast, put the sausages and mushrooms in the air fryer and brush lightly with olive oil. Air fry for 5 minutes at 200°C. Remove the tray, turn the sausages and mushrooms over, then return to the air fryer, still at 200°C, for a further 3 minutes. Place the bacon and tomatoes on top. Spray or brush the tomatoes lightly with olive oil and season with sea salt and cracked black pepper. Return the tray to the air fryer at 200°C for 6 minutes.

For the spinach, put a frying pan over a medium heat, add the butter and melt, then add the spinach and cook for around 90 seconds until wilted. Put the spinach in a colander to drain any excess water, then season with salt and pepper.

To serve, cook two eggs to your liking (scrambled, fried, poached, etc). Place the toasted wholemeal and rye toast on a plate and spread with butter. Top with the spinach, mushrooms, tomatoes, sausages and bacon. Add the eggs and garnish with parsley.

This pie is so delicious we had to include it even though the all-butter pastry is indulgent; we believe in everything in moderation, so we've only put the pastry on top and balanced the dish with an abundance of tender and tasty protein-packed chicken as well as broccoli and peas which are fantastic sources of fibre.

CHICKEN, BACON AND LEEK PIE WITH PURPLE SPROUTING BROCCOLI, PEAS AND PARSLEY BUTTER

Nutritional information

Amount per serving	
Protein	51.0g
Fat	65.4g
Carbohydrates	39.9g
Fibre	9.1g
Energy	934kcal

Serves: 6
Prep time: 30 minutes
Cooking time: 45 minutes

for the chicken pie
50g butter
1 small onion, *peeled and chopped*
100g dry-cured air-dried bacon lardons
sea salt and cracked black pepper
2 cloves of garlic, *peeled and chopped*
400g chicken breast, *diced*
400g chicken thigh, *diced*
1 leek, *trimmed and diced*
1 tbsp plain flour
2 sprigs of thyme, *leaves only, chopped*
1 chicken stock cube, *crumbled*
200ml double cream
2 bunches of asparagus, *cut into 1-inch lengths*
2 tbsps wholegrain mustard
1 pack of all-butter puff pastry
1 large free-range egg, *beaten (for the egg wash)*
3g yellow mustard seeds
1g dried parsley

for the vegetables
25g butter at room temperature
zest of ½ a lemon
10g parsley, *leaves only, chopped*
sea salt and cracked black pepper
400g purple sprouting broccoli
400g frozen peas

For the chicken pie, preheat the oven to 180°C/350°F/gas mark 4. Place a heavy-based saucepan over a medium heat and melt the butter. Add the onion, bacon, salt, pepper and garlic. Sweat down until the onions are soft and light golden. Add the chicken and fry until golden brown. Add the leek and cook until it starts to soften (around a minute), then de-glaze the pan with a splash of water. Add the flour, thyme, more salt and pepper and cook for a further minute whilst constantly stirring so the flour does not burn. Add the stock cube and cream and cook, stirring continually, until the sauce bubbles and becomes thick. Add the asparagus and mustard then transfer to a pie tin and allow to cool down completely. Meanwhile cut a rough circle of puff pastry, around 15mm bigger than your pie tin. Eggwash the edge of the pie tin and cut some of the leftover pastry into 15mm strips to line the edge of the pie tin. Place the pastry lid on top of the pie, pressing down the edges to seal the lid. Make a decorative crimp using your fingers or a fork. Brush the whole pie twice with egg wash and then gently sprinkle the mustard seeds and dried parsley over the pie lid. Place in the oven for 35 minutes until the pastry is golden brown.

For the vegetables, make a parsley butter by mixing the butter, lemon zest, parsley, salt and pepper; set aside. Bring a pan of water with a pinch of salt to the boil and blanch the broccoli and peas for 1-2 minutes (they should still have a bite); drain well. Place in a pre-heated serving bowl and dot with the parsley butter then serve immediately with the pie.

The star of this recipe is undoubtedly the dry-cured, air-dried gammon, expertly produced by our food hero Chris Battle using his family's cure. The air-drying process allows the gammon to mature over two to three weeks, developing the flavour and allowing the salt to dissipate, leaving a mild and beautifully balanced gammon. The creaminess of the vegetable gratin works beautifully with the meaty texture of the gammon.

CRACKLING GAMMON JOINT WITH MARMALADE GLAZE, PAN-FRIED SPROUTS, PEAS AND BACON, AND VEGETABLE GRATIN

Nutritional information

Amount per serving	
Protein	60.8g
Fat	32.8g
Carbohydrates	36.7g
Fibre	7.3g
Energy	674kcal

Serves: 10
Prep time: 20 minutes
Cooking time: 90 minutes

for the vegetable gratin
50g butter
50g plain flour
500ml whole milk
150g grated Gruyère cheese
150g grated Cheddar cheese
1 tsp Dijon mustard
1 cauliflower
200g stem broccoli
200g kale, chopped
80g breadcrumbs

for the marmalade glaze
100g orange marmalade
50ml water
1 English breakfast tea bag

for the crackling gammon
1.5kg air-dried rind-on, boneless gammon joint
1 tsp vegetable oil
1 tsp table salt

for the sprouts, peas and bacon
1 tbsp sunflower oil
60g smoked bacon lardons
600g Brussels sprouts, *trimmed and halved*
400g frozen peas

For the vegetable gratin, add the butter to a pan over a low heat and melt, add the flour and stir to combine. Cook for a minute before adding the milk a little at a time, constantly stirring to ensure a smooth sauce. Bring to a simmer then add the cheeses and Dijon mustard, reserving a little cheese for topping at the end. Remove from the heat and stir until the cheese has melted. Cut the cauliflower into small florets and blanch in a pan of boiling salted water for 4-5 minutes. Drain and place in a large casserole dish along with the stem broccoli and kale. Pour over the cheese sauce and cover with foil before baking for 30 minutes at 180°C/350°F/gas mark 4. Scatter over the breadcrumbs and reserved cheese before baking for a further 10 minutes until golden.

For the marmalade glaze, add the orange marmalade and water to a medium saucepan and gently heat until the marmalade melts then cut open the tea bag and add the contents to the pan, discarding the bag. Remove from the heat and allow to steep for at least 15 minutes.

For the crackling gammon, preheat the oven to 220°C/425°F/gas mark 7. Place the gammon on a baking tray, wrap the sides and bottom of the joint in tin foil leaving the rind exposed at the top. Brush the rind with a teaspoon of vegetable oil and season with the salt. Cook for 30 minutes, until the rind crackles, then decrease the temperature to 180°C and cook for a further hour. Using a meat thermometer, check the centre of the gammon has reached 68°C before removing to rest for at least 15 minutes.

For the sprouts, peas and bacon, add the oil, bacon lardons and sprouts to a frying pan over a medium heat and fry for 5-6 minutes until the bacon and sprouts are golden brown. Add the frozen peas and cook for another 90 seconds.

To serve, carve the gammon and arrange on plates before pouring over the warm marmalade glaze at the last minute. Serve the vegetable gratin and sprouts, peas and bacon alongside.

Our Duroc pork is specifically bred for its high levels of marbling fat and mouth-wateringly flavoursome tender pork. The tomapork is a thicker pork chop with the bone left in and a longer 'tail', where all the flavour resides – a porky take on a tomahawk beef steak. Don't overcook it and it will be deliciously juicy! The Argentinian chimichurri sauce lends a touch of fusion to this dish, its tangy freshness really complements the pork. The air fryer chips are a lighter alternative to the norm.

PAN-SEARED DUROC TOMAPORK WITH CHIMICHURRI SAUCE AND TWICE-COOKED AIR FRYER CHIPS

Nutritional information

Amount per serving	
Protein	51.9g
Fat	44.0g
Carbohydrates	35.3g
Fibre	8.4g
Energy	729kcal

Serves: 4
Prep time: 30 minutes
Cooking time: 30 minutes

for the chips
500g Maris Piper potatoes, *unpeeled*
vegetable oil
sea salt and cracked black pepper

for the tomapork
2 Duroc tomapork steaks
10ml vegetable oil
20g salted butter
3 sprigs rosemary
3 sprigs thyme
2 garlic cloves, *peeled and crushed*
sea salt and cracked black pepper

for the broccoli
300g stem broccoli
2 cloves garlic, *peeled and finely sliced*
1 tbsp extra virgin olive oil
sea salt and cracked black pepper

for the chimichurri
100g fresh parsley, *thick stalks removed*
½ tsp dried oregano
juice and zest of 1 lime
juice of 1 lemon
5g red pepper flakes
40ml red wine vinegar
50ml olive oil
3 garlic cloves, *peeled and finely chopped*
1 fresh red chilli, *finely chopped*
sea salt and cracked black pepper

for the tomatoes
1 punnet cherry tomatoes, on the vine
10ml olive oil
sea salt and cracked black pepper

for the garnish
1 bag washed lamb's lettuce

For the chips, square off the potatoes by trimming all 4 edges. Cut the potatoes in half lengthways, then cut each half into 2 or 3 chips. Repeat until you have cut all the potatoes. Place into a large pan and fill with cold water. Bring up to a rolling boil and blanch the chips for 6-8 minutes, or until you can easily pierce the centre of the chips with the tip of a knife. Drain the chips and spread out onto a tray lined with paper towel to dry, ensuring they aren't touching each other. Preheat the air fryer to 200°C. Put the dried chips in a bowl and coat with vegetable oil, ensuring even coverage. Put into the air fryer for around 20 minutes, or until the desired colour and crunch has been achieved. Remove from the air fryer and season with cracked black pepper and sea salt.

For the tomapork, remove the steaks from the fridge and packaging at least 30 minutes before you begin to cook to allow them to come up to room temperature. Preheat a frying pan on high with the vegetable oil, and preheat your oven to 180°C/350°F/gas mark 4. Add the steaks to the pan, cook on the fat edge for 2 minutes, then a further 2 minutes on each side. Add the butter, herbs, garlic, salt and pepper and baste for another minute. Place on a foil-lined baking tray and cook in the oven for 6 minutes; turn over and cook for another 6 minutes. Check the thickest part of the meat with a meat thermometer; you need a core temperature of 68°C. Cover in foil and rest for 2 minutes.

For the broccoli, place a griddle pan on to a medium-to-high heat. Toss the broccoli and garlic with the olive oil and season well. When the pan is hot, add the broccoli and cook for 90 seconds; flip each piece and cook for another 90 seconds.

For the chimichurri, place all the ingredients into a food processor and blitz to a smooth sauce. Season to taste with sea salt and cracked black pepper.

For the tomatoes, place the tomatoes on a baking tray, brush with a little oil and season with salt and cracked black pepper. Place in the oven with the tomaporks for 4-5 minutes until the tomato skins start to split.

To serve, with a sharp knife, remove the bone that runs down the side of the tomapork and cut the steak into 1cm thick slices. Spoon over the chimichurri and serve with the broccoli, tomatoes, lamb's lettuce and chips.

We're well known for our sausages and we make the very best, using whole cuts of outdoor-bred British pork shoulder and belly, coarsely chopped and gently blended with fresh herbs and authentic ingredients, as pioneered by our food hero Martin Heap back in 1995. This dish is a British classic: a real winter warmer. The peas and leeks are a fantastic source of fibre and the addition of balsamic vinegar to the gravy gives a delicious finish.

PROPER SAUSAGE AND MASH WITH CRISPY LEEKS AND RED ONION GRAVY

Nutritional information

Amount per serving	
Protein	33.0g
Fat	55.1g
Carbohydrates	49.5g
Fibre	11.2g
Energy	842kcal

Serves: 4
Prep time: 10 minutes
Cooking time: 35 minutes

for the mash
600g King Edward potatoes, *peeled and quartered*
sea salt and cracked black pepper
40g unsalted butter
40ml double cream

for the crispy leeks
vegetable oil
½ leek

for the sausages
vegetable oil
8 premium pork sausages in natural hog casings

for the gravy
½ tbsp vegetable oil
1 large red onion, *peeled and finely sliced*
2 garlic cloves, *peeled and finely diced*
80ml red wine
20ml balsamic vinegar
2 sprigs of thyme
400ml chicken stock
20g plain flour
30g water

for the vegetables
1 tbsp vegetable oil
1 leek, *trimmed and cut into 1cm rounds*
200g frozen petit pois peas
50ml water
20g unsalted butter
5g fresh mint, *stalks removed and finely sliced*
sea salt and cracked black pepper

For the mash, place the potatoes in a large saucepan and cover with cold water; season with sea salt. Place over a high heat and bring to the boil. Once boiling reduce to a medium heat and simmer the potatoes for 20-30 minutes until soft. Drain and add the butter and double cream. Mash together until the potato is silky smooth. Season with sea salt and cracked black pepper.

For the crispy leeks, in a frying pan over a medium-to-high heat, add enough vegetable oil to shallow fry the leeks. Trim the leek and cut into roughly 10-12cm long pieces, then cut each piece in half lengthways. Place the flat side down on your chopping board and slice as finely as possible. Consistently fine strips of leeks will mean you have super crispy leeks after cooking. In small batches fry the leeks until crispy; remove from the oil and place into a bowl lined with kitchen roll to soak up any excess oil.

For the sausages, place a frying pan on the hob on a medium-to-high heat. When hot add 1 tablespoon of vegetable oil and add the sausages. Turn the sausages every 45 seconds until golden brown on all sides. Be careful not to split the skins (or pierce with a fork) as this will allow more juices to escape resulting in a less succulent eating sausage.

For the gravy, add the vegetable oil, onion and garlic to a frying pan over a medium-to-high heat. Fry until starting to turn golden brown. Add the red wine, balsamic vinegar and thyme and cook until nearly all the liquid has gone and it looks like a thick syrup. Add the chicken stock and bring to the boil, reduce the heat to medium and reduce the stock by half. Mix the flour and water together then stir quickly into the gravy to make a double cream-like consistency of gravy. Simmer for 5 minutes before removing the thyme and serving.

For the vegetables, add the vegetable oil and leek rounds to a frying pan over a medium-to-high heat and cook until the leeks are caramelised on one side; flip over to caramelise on the other. Add the peas and water and cook for 1 minute, turning occasionally. Add the butter and mint and season with sea salt and cracked black pepper. Make sure the butter is melted before you remove from the heat.

To serve, place a generous spoon of mash in the centre of each plate, add the vegetables and top with two pork sausages. Pour some gravy over, then add the crispy fried leek on top of the sausages.

ROAST PORK WITH CRISPY CRACKLING, HONEY-ROASTED ROOT VEGETABLES, YORKSHIRE PUDDINGS AND RED WINE GRAVY

Nutritional information

Amount per serving	
Protein	55.5g
Fat	39.4g
Carbohydrates	56.0g
Fibre	6.5g
Energy	817kcal

Serves: 6
Prep time: 30 minutes
Cooking time: 90 minutes

for the pork
1-1.2kg rind-on boneless pork loin joint, *straight scored*
table salt
1 tsp vegetable oil

for the Yorkshire puddings
6 eggs
500ml whole milk
200g plain flour
sea salt
6 tsps vegetable oil

for the gravy
150ml red wine
50ml balsamic vinegar
2 sprigs of thyme
600ml chicken stock
30g plain flour
50ml water

for the roast potatoes
400g red potatoes, *peeled and cut in half*
3 tbsps sunflower oil
8 cloves garlic, *peeled*
10g fresh thyme
15g fresh rosemary
sea salt and cracked black pepper

for the root vegetables
200g red beetroots, *peeled and quartered*
400g chantenay carrots, *tops removed*
200g baby shallots, *peeled*
1 tbsp extra virgin olive oil
10g fresh thyme
4 cloves garlic, *peeled and sliced*
sea salt and cracked black pepper
2 tbsps blossom honey

for the French beans
200g French beans, *topped and tailed*
10g unsalted butter
sea salt and cracked black pepper

For the pork, place the pork on a wire rack on a thick baking tray. Pat the rind dry with kitchen towel and then generously cover with table salt, ensuring it's rubbed into the scores on the rind. For best results do this the night before, or at least half an hour before cooking. If preparing the night before, once salted return to the fridge, uncovered if possible, to dry out the rind overnight.

Preheat your oven to 220°C/425°F/gas mark 7. Dry the rind again with a paper towel then brush lightly with vegetable oil and re-sprinkle generously with table salt. Place in the oven for 25 minutes until the crackling has popped and turned golden brown. Turn the oven down to 180°C/350°F/gas mark 4 for 30-45 minutes until the pork has reached a core temperature of 68°C. Remove from the oven, loosely cover with tin foil to rest for at least 20 minutes before serving.

For the Yorkshire puddings, whisk the eggs, milk and flour together until a smooth batter has formed, seasoning with salt only. Put a teaspoon of vegetable oil into each cup of a Yorkshire pudding tray and place in the centre of the oven until the oil is smoking hot. Remove the tray and pour in the batter to fill ¾ of each cup. Place back in the oven and cook for 18 minutes; once the puddings have risen and browned consistently, turn down the oven to 180°C/350°F/gas mark 4 and cook for a further 10 minutes. Remove from the oven once crisp and set aside.

For the gravy, add the red wine, balsamic vinegar and thyme to a saucepan over a medium-to-high heat and cook until the liquid has evaporated by half and looks like a thick syrup. Add the chicken stock and bring to the boil. Turn down the heat to medium and reduce the stock by half; this should take 15-20 minutes. Mix the flour and water together then stir quickly into the gravy to make a double cream-like consistency. Simmer for 5 minutes before removing the thyme and serving.

For the roast potatoes, add the potatoes to a pan of salted water and parboil them until a knife can reach the centre with a little force; this should take 8-10 minutes. Drain and toss in a colander until the sides have become fluffy; this will give the potatoes perfect crisp edges once roasted. Place them on a baking tray and drizzle over the sunflower oil, add the garlic, thyme and rosemary and season well with salt and pepper. Place in the oven at 180°C/350°F/gas mark 4 for 35-40 minutes until golden and crispy.

For the root vegetables, place the beetroots, carrots and shallots into a roasting tray. Drizzle with oil and season with the fresh thyme, garlic and salt and pepper. Drizzle over two tablespoons of honey and place in the pre-heated oven at 180°C/350°F/gas mark 4 for 40 minutes, turning halfway through.

For the French beans, bring a small pan of water to the boil over a medium-to-high heat, drop in the beans carefully and boil for 90 seconds. Drain, add the butter and season well with sea salt and cracked black pepper.

To serve, carve the pork into slices with the crackling and serve with a jug of hot gravy, Yorkshire puddings, root vegetables, green beans and roast potatoes.

This recipe is a brilliant take on modern British BBQ. Not only will it show you how to make mouth-wateringly crispy crackling on the BBQ, but also the addition of wood chunks enhances the smoky flavour in the juicy meat and vegetables. Paired with smoked beets, fennel and broccoli, cooked on the BBQ and served with a blueberry and pomegranate vinaigrette, this dish is a superfood feast in disguise!

ROAST RACK OF BBQ PORK WITH CRISPY CRACKLING, SMOKED VEGETABLES AND BLUEBERRY VINAIGRETTE

Nutritional information

Amount per serving	
Protein	37.3g
Fat	43.0g
Carbohydrates	27.7g
Fibre	8.1g
Energy	632kcal

Serves: 6
Prep time: 20 minutes
Cooking time: 90 minutes

for the pork
1.2kg pork rib roast
table salt
1 tsp vegetable oil

for the vegetables
2 bulbs of fennel, *diced into 3cm pieces*
12 small raw beetroots, *washed and quartered*
500g purple sprouting broccoli
1 tbsp extra virgin olive oil
5g fresh thyme stalks
sea salt and cracked black pepper
zest of 1 lemon

for the vinaigrette
150g blueberries
30ml cider vinegar
20ml balsamic vinegar
30ml extra virgin olive oil
1 tbsp Dijon mustard
20g honey
sea salt and cracked black pepper
1 pomegranate, *seeds only*

for the garnish
10g fresh parsley leaves

For the pork, place the pork joint onto a baking tray. Sprinkle some salt over the rind and leave at room temperature for 1 hour. Set up your kettle BBQ using the indirect method, see page 173, to 200°C-220°C. Once you have a stable temperature, add two oak wood chunks of wood to start smoking for flavour. Wipe the rind of the pork with kitchen roll, lightly brush the top with vegetable oil and re-salt the rind. Place the rib in the BBQ directly on the cooking grate, close the lid and leave to cook for 35 minutes. Check the pork: the crackling should have bubbled and turned a lovely golden-brown colour. Close off the bottom vents so they are only slightly open to start to reduce the temperature in the BBQ to 160°C -170°C and cook for a further 35 minutes. Using a meat thermometer, check the thickest part of the meat: you are looking for a temperature of 68°C. Remove the joint from the BBQ, cover loosely with foil and allow to rest for at least 20 minutes.

For the vegetables, mix all the vegetables in a bowl and add the oil, thyme and seasoning and mix. Place onto an oven tray and put into the BBQ when you have reduced the temperature to 160-170°C. Cook the vegetables for 35-45 minutes until tender. Remove from the BBQ and grate over the lemon zest.

For the vinaigrette, in a blender add half of the blueberries, the vinegars, olive oil, Dijon mustard and honey. Season with sea salt and cracked black pepper and blend for 30 seconds. Pour into a bowl, add the remaining blueberries and pomegranate seeds and mix.

To serve, slice the pork rib roast in between the bones and place one onto each plate. Add a generous spoon of smoked vegetables and drizzle over the vinaigrette. Garnish with fresh parsley.

Superfoods are nutrient-rich foods considered to be especially beneficial for health and well-being, so they're super-healthy and delicious. This recipe is bursting with the flavour and colour of superfoods like blueberries, edamame beans and beetroot and the crispy quinoa adds a delightful crunch. The chicken couldn't be easier to cook perfectly in the air fryer with a little olive oil, garlic and thyme.

SUPERFOOD SALAD WITH CRISPY QUINOA AND AIR FRYER CHICKEN

For the dressing, add the lemon juice and zest to the coconut yoghurt, season with sea salt and cracked black pepper and whisk together until combined. Set aside in the fridge.

For the crispy quinoa, add the cooked quinoa to a mixing bowl and drizzle over extra virgin olive oil, a pinch of sea salt and cracked black pepper. Place the quinoa in the air fryer, make sure it's evenly spread and cook for 13-15 minutes at 200°C until crisp, shaking the basket after 8 minutes. Set aside for later to garnish the salad.

For the salad, bring a pan of water to the boil, then carefully add the broccoli and cook for 90 seconds. Immediately spoon the broccoli into a bowl of cold water to stop it cooking and keep it really green. Remove from the water, drain, place in a bowl and cover with cling film. Set aside in the fridge.

Place the butternut squash into the air fryer, season with extra virgin olive oil, sea salt and cracked black pepper and cook for 10 minutes at 200°C until the squash has started to colour. Set aside in the fridge.

Roughly chop the cos lettuce and add to a bowl with the remaining ingredients. Drizzle on extra virgin olive oil, season with sea salt and cracked black pepper and gently toss the salad until combined.

For the chicken, place the chicken breasts in the air fryer and season with extra virgin olive oil, sea salt, grated garlic and fresh thyme. Cook for 18 minutes at 180°C, turning after 10 minutes. Check the chicken with a temperature probe: it should read 72°C and the juices should run clear. Let the chicken rest for 5 minutes.

While the chicken rests, add the broccoli and squash to the salad.

To serve, slice the chicken breasts into thick slices and place on the salad, drizzle with the coconut yoghurt dressing and the crispy quinoa over the top.

Nutritional information

Amount per serving	
Protein	41.9g
Fat	18.4g
Carbohydrates	62.1g
Fibre	9.5g
Energy	669kcal

Serves: 4
Prep time: 5 minutes
Cooking time: 25 minutes

for the dressing
zest and juice of 1 lemon
200g coconut yoghurt
sea salt and cracked black pepper

for the crispy quinoa
100g ready-cooked quinoa
1 tbsp extra virgin olive oil
sea salt and cracked black pepper

for the salad
200g stem broccoli, *stalks trimmed*
300g butternut squash, *peeled and diced*
2 tsps extra virgin olive oil
sea salt and cracked black pepper
1 cos lettuce, *washed and roughly chopped*
100g of baby leaf salad leaves
100g fresh blueberries
250g ready-to-eat spelt
100g golden raisins
100g ready-to-eat edamame beans
50g pomegranate seeds
100g vine cherry tomatoes, *stalks removed and cut in half*
150g cooked beetroot, *quartered*
1 large carrot, *peeled and sliced into fine batons*

for the chicken
2 large chicken breasts
1 tsp extra virgin olive oil
sea salt
2 garlic cloves, *peeled and finely grated*
5g fresh thyme, *stalks removed*

Another classic! Yorkshire pudding has been on British tables since the 18th century when batter puddings were created to help the meat – the most expensive part of the meal – go further. The key to making the puddings rise is to trust the process: don't be tempted to open the oven door too soon.

TOAD IN THE HOLE WITH ROASTED WINTER ROOT VEGETABLES, WHOLEGRAIN MUSTARD AND BEER GRAVY

Nutritional information

Amount per serving	
Protein	37.7g
Fat	48.5g
Carbohydrates	54.2g
Fibre	9.6g
Energy	817kcal

Serves: 6
Prep time: 15-20 minutes
Cooking time: 25 minutes

for the roasted vegetables
3 large carrots, *peeled and cut into batons*
1 bunch raw beetroot, *peeled and cut into wedges*
400g butternut squash, *peeled and cut into 2cm chunks*
1 tbsp extra virgin olive oil
50g honey
5g fresh thyme
sea salt and cracked black pepper
200g stem broccoli

for the gravy
½ tbsp vegetable oil
1 large red onion, *peeled and finely sliced*
2 garlic cloves, *peeled and finely diced*
200ml IPA beer
20ml balsamic vinegar
2 sprigs of thyme, *leaves only*
300ml chicken stock
300ml beef stock
20g plain flour
50g wholegrain mustard
40ml water
1 tbsp brown sauce

for the toad in the hole
4 large eggs
150g plain flour
265ml milk
sea salt
4 tbsps sunflower oil
12 premium pork sausages in hog casings

For the roasted vegetables, preheat the oven to 200°C/400°F/gas mark 6. Place the vegetables (except the broccoli) into a bowl. Add the olive oil, honey, thyme, sea salt and cracked black pepper and gently toss. Spread the vegetables out on a baking tray ready to go in the oven.

For the gravy, add the vegetable oil, onion and garlic to a frying pan over a medium-to-high heat. Fry until starting to turn golden brown. Add the beer, balsamic vinegar and thyme and cook until the liquid has reduced to a thick syrup. Add the stocks and bring to the boil. Reduce the heat to medium and reduce the stock again by half. Mix the flour, mustard and water together then stir in quickly to make a gravy the consistency of double cream. Simmer for 5 minutes before finishing with 1 tablespoon of brown sauce.

For the toad in the hole, whisk the eggs, flour and milk together to form a smooth batter, seasoning with salt only. Put 4 tablespoons of sunflower oil into a deep baking tray and put into the pre-heated oven for 5 minutes. Carefully take the tray out of the oven and pour in all the batter, adding the sausages with space in between them. Place the tray back into the oven along with the vegetable tray and cook for 25 minutes. After 20 minutes take out the vegetables, add the stem broccoli and mix carefully together. Return to the oven for a further 5 minutes. *Chef's tip:* do not open the oven for at least 20 minutes or the Yorkshire pudding batter will not rise properly.

To serve, take the toad in the hole out of the oven, set aside to rest, check the vegetables to make sure they are nicely cooked and roasted. Portion up the toad in the hole and serve with the roasted veg and a good helping of beer and mustard gravy.

Cotoletta di pollo with new potatoes and salsa verde – *Italian*

Chicken gyros with Greek salad and feta tzatziki – *Greek*

Chicken shawarma with houmous and charred aubergine – *Middle Eastern*

Emilia Romagna antipasti board – *Italian*

Feijoada sausage stew – *Portuguese*

Grilled BBQ chicken with charred vegetables, new potatoes and smoked garlic pesto – *Italian*

Harissa roast chicken, couscous, baba ghanoush and roasted spiced cauliflower – *Tunisian*

Honey and ras el hanout BBQ chicken with pomegranate salad and mint yogurt – *Moroccan*

Iberian paella – *Spanish*

Ibérico cheese tortilla with chorizo, Serrano ham, Spanish baked beans and wild rocket – *Spanish*

Ibérico pork presa with mojo rojo sauce, patatas bravas and charred broccoli – *Spanish*

Jamón Ibérico and scrambled eggs – *Spanish*

Niçoise salad with air fryer butterfly chicken – *French*

Pork ragù with fresh bronze die fusilli gigante pasta – *Italian*

Pork saltimbocca – *Italian*

Roast leg of lamb with whipped feta, flatbreads, tomato and apricot salad, and houmous – *Greek*

Shakshuka with chicken, feta and spiced crispy chickpeas – *Tunisian*

MEDITERRANEAN

Mediterranean cuisine is simpl
ingredients and widely know
The Mediterranean climate yields a
dairy, fruits, vegetables, legumes an
life rather than a diet and the ac
the experience, providing socia
enjoyment as well as th

ased on fresh and locally produced
be a healthy way of eating.
oundance of wholesome foods; meat,
f course, olive oil. Food is a way of
f eating together is fundamental to
nd psychological benefits through
utritional benefit of food

I have an Italian wife, so this recipe is a staple in my house. However, I've made one fundamental tweak to this otherwise authentic Italian dish. Traditionally the chicken would be flattened to make it very large and thin. But this uses a lot of extra breadcrumbs, which pick up more oil, so I've left the chicken quite thick, which also keeps it more juicy and succulent.

COTOLETTA DI POLLO WITH NEW POTATOES AND SALSA VERDE

For the cotoletta, place each chicken breast between two double thicknesses of cling film. Using a rolling pin or meat mallet, beat the chicken until it's about 1cm thick - it will be about double its original size. Take 3 bowls, add the plain flour to one (seasoned with sea salt and cracked black pepper), add the beaten egg to the second bowl and the breadcrumbs to the third. Prepare a line on your kitchen worktop: flattened chicken, flour, egg, breadcrumbs and finally an empty tray for the finished coated chicken. Take each chicken breast and fully coat in flour, egg and finally breadcrumbs. Shake off any excess and place on the empty tray.

For the new potatoes, place the potatoes in the air fryer. Slice off the base of the garlic bulb and separate the cloves but leave the skin on; add to the potatoes. Drizzle with extra virgin olive oil and season with sea salt and cracked black pepper and sprigs of fresh rosemary. Air fry at 200°C for 25-30 minutes, mixing after 15 minutes.

For the salsa verde, in a blender add the herbs, garlic, oil, red wine vinegar, Dijon mustard and capers and season with sea salt and cracked black pepper. Blend to a smooth sauce.

To fry the cotoletta, in a large frying pan on a medium-to-high heat, add enough vegetable oil to shallow fry the chicken. Drop in a couple of leftover breadcrumbs to see if the oil is hot enough; they should start to sizzle immediately. Carefully place in one of the cotoletta and fry for around 2 minutes or until golden brown; turn over and repeat. When golden brown on both sides, remove from the pan and place onto a tray lined with kitchen roll to soak up any residual oil. If you have a meat thermometer, check that the chicken is over 72°C in the centre of the thickest part of the meat. Top up the oil if needed and repeat with the next three cotoletta.

To serve, in a bowl toss the salad leaves, tomatoes and olives with some extra virgin olive oil and season with salt and pepper. Place the cotoletta on four plates, season and finely grate over some lemon zest. Add some potatoes and salad to each plate and drizzle some salsa verde over the cotoletta. Quarter the lemon used for zest and add a wedge to each plate for squeezing over the meat.

Nutritional information

Amount per serving	
Protein	38.3g
Fat	40.3g
Carbohydrates	65.5g
Fibre	8.0g
Energy	763kcal

Serves: 4
Prep time: 20 minutes
Cooking time: 30 minutes

for the cotoletta
4 small chicken breasts
60g plain flour
sea salt and cracked black pepper
2 eggs, *beaten*
160g white breadcrumbs
vegetable oil

for the new potatoes
360g mini new potatoes
1 bulb of garlic
2 tbsps extra virgin olive oil
sea salt and cracked black pepper
10g fresh rosemary

for the salsa verde
40g flat leaf parsley
10g basil
2 garlic cloves, *peeled*
90g extra virgin olive oil
30ml red wine vinegar
2 tsps Dijon mustard
15g capers, drained
sea salt and cracked black pepper

for the garnish
1 bag mixed leaf salad leaves
4 Italian vine tomatoes, *quartered*
140g pitted nocellara olives
extra virgin olive oil
sea salt and cracked black pepper
1 lemon

Greek and Cypriot eating is recognised for its healthy, tasty and simple dishes which allow the ingredients to shine. This dish is traditionally cooked on a vertical rotisserie and served on a pitta bread. It can be made with pork, chicken or beef. This is a traditional recipe with a simple but tasty twist to the classic tzatziki – the addition of feta blended into the recipe. This gives it another layer of flavour with sour and salty notes coming through as well as the fresh Greek yoghurt, mint and dill. Any leftovers are great the next day as a salad dressing.

CHICKEN GYROS WITH GREEK SALAD AND FETA TZATZIKI

For the chicken gyros, in a bowl combine the chicken, yogurt, olive oil, lemon juice, garlic, shallots, paprika, oregano, red pepper flakes, cumin, coriander, white wine vinegar and a large pinch each of salt and pepper. Cover and marinate for at least 15 minutes at room temperature, preferably 3 hours in the fridge or, for best results, overnight.

Preheat the oven to 200°C/400°F/gas mark 6. Place the chicken on a baking tray. Cook for 15 minutes then turn and cook for another 10 minutes. Using a meat thermometer, check the chicken has reached 80°C in the thickest part of the meat. Remove the chicken from the oven and place onto a cutting board. Cover with tin foil and allow to rest for 5 minutes, then slice thinly.

For the feta tzatziki, put the feta, half of the yogurt, the garlic and lemon juice in a blender and blend until creamy. Stir in the rest of the yogurt, the grated cucumber, dill, mint and a pinch of sea salt and cracked black pepper.

For the Greek salad, in a bowl mix all of the ingredients together with the olive oil and season with sea salt and cracked black pepper.

To serve, spread each pitta or flatbread with feta tzatziki and top with shredded lettuce, Greek salad and finally the thinly sliced chicken. Drizzle over some more feta tzatziki and sprinkle with dill and mint leaves. Season with a squeeze of fresh lemon, sea salt and cracked black pepper.

Nutritional information

Amount per serving	
Protein	41.9g
Fat	26.3g
Carbohydrates	40.8g
Fibre	5.9g
Energy	558kcal

Serves: 4
Prep time: 20 minutes, *plus up to 24 hours marinating time*
Cooking time: 25 minutes

for the chicken gyros
500g chicken thighs, boneless and skinless
85g full fat Greek yogurt
1 tbsp extra virgin olive oil
1 tbsp fresh lemon juice
3 garlic cloves, *peeled and finely diced*
2 shallots, *peeled and finely diced*
1 tbsp smoked paprika
1 tbsp dried oregano
1 tsp red pepper flakes
1 tsp ground cumin
1 tsp ground coriander
1 tbsp white wine vinegar
sea salt and cracked black pepper

for the feta tzatziki
100g feta cheese
200g full fat Greek yogurt
1 garlic clove, peeled and grated
juice of 1 small lemon
1 cucumber, *halved, seeds removed and grated*
1 tbsp fresh dill, chopped
½ tbsp fresh mint leaves, *chopped*
sea salt and cracked black pepper

for the Greek salad
2 vine tomatoes, *quartered, seeds removed and diced*
1 cucumber, *halved, seeds removed and diced*
1 small red onion, *peeled and finely diced*
10g fresh dill, *finely chopped*
5g fresh mint leaves, *finely chopped*
50g Halkidiki olives, *pitted and sliced*
1 tbsp extra virgin olive oil
sea salt and cracked black pepper

for the wrap
4 pitta breads or flatbreads

for the garnish
1 lemon, *cut into quarters*
½ iceberg lettuce, *washed and shredded*
15g fresh dill, *chopped*
10g fresh mint leaves

Chicken shawarma originated in modern day Turkey and is eaten throughout the Arab world, as well as becoming popular in the West in recent years. This take makes it really easy to cook: no rotating spit required! You could always add a warm flatbread to create something more 'street food' than 'sit down' meal. The houmous is a key part of this dish, not just a dip, as is traditional.

CHICKEN SHAWARMA WITH HOUMOUS AND CHARRED AUBERGINE

For the marinade, mix all the ingredients in a bowl. Add the chicken thighs and mix until the meat is well coated. Place into the fridge for at least 30 minutes; 2 hours is ideal.

For the aubergines, preheat the oven to 200°C/400°F/gas mark 6. Slice the aubergines in half lengthways. Carefully, without piercing the skin, score the flesh in a diamond pattern. Place onto a baking tray, skin side down, drizzle each half with a tablespoon of olive oil and season with salt and pepper. Roast in the oven for 20-25 minutes until the flesh is soft and golden brown.

To fry the chicken, preheat a pan on a medium heat with the sunflower oil and fry the chicken thighs for 7-8 minutes on each side or until the meat is cooked through – use a meat thermometer to check that the thickest part of the meat has reached 80°C. Remove from the heat, cover with foil and rest for 3 minutes.

To serve, place a half aubergine on each plate. Spoon a bed of houmous alongside. Slice the chicken into 2cm slices and lay on top of the houmous. Garnish each plate with coriander and a sprinkling of pomegranate seeds.

Nutritional information

Amount per serving	
Protein	45.6g
Fat	45.3g
Carbohydrates	25.2g
Fibre	10.5g
Energy	670kcal

Serves: 4
Prep time: 10 minutes,
plus up to 2 hours marinating time
Cooking time: 30 minutes

for the marinade
1 tbsp sea salt
½ tsp cracked black pepper
1 tsp ground cumin
1 tsp dried coriander
1 tsp smoked paprika
½ tsp ground cloves
1 tsp cayenne pepper
1 tsp ground cinnamon
2 garlic cloves, *peeled and finely grated*
zest and juice of 1 lemon
2 tbsps plain yoghurt

for the chicken
600g boneless skinless chicken thighs
1tbsp sunflower oil

for the aubergines
2 large aubergines
4 tbsps extra virgin olive oil
sea salt and cracked black pepper

to garnish
200g RAMONA'S houmous
25g fresh coriander leaves
80g pomegranate seeds

Antipasti roughly translates in Italian to 'before the meal' and has become a popular appetiser all over the world. An antipasti board is different to a charcuterie or salumi board as it contains more than just meat. This board features Italian favourites such as Nocellara del Belice olives, stuffed peppers, focaccia and Parmigiano Reggiano (served in chunks as the Italians do) as well as five wonderful examples of Italian salumi, including one of the most famous, prosciutto di Parma, the king of hams.

EMILIA ROMAGNA ANTIPASTI BOARD

For the antipasti board, gently separate the slices of meat and arrange them on a large wooden platter or board. Place three small bowls around the board and fill them with the olives, stuffed peppers and the chunks of Parmigiano Reggiano. Place the mozzarella and tomatoes around the board.

To serve, preheat the oven to 180°C/350°F/gas mark 4. Place the focaccia on a tray, drizzle with 1 tablespoon of extra virgin olive oil and place in the oven for 4-5 minutes to warm. Remove from the oven and cut into 6 equal slices. Place the rocket into a bowl and add 1 tablespoon of extra virgin olive oil, tossing to cover all the leaves. Garnish the antipasti board with your dressed rocket and using a fine grater, grate the Parmigiano Reggiano over the top.

Nutritional information

Amount per serving	
Protein	35.9g
Fat	72.5g
Carbohydrates	42.9g
Fibre	4.6g
Energy	662kcal

Serves: 6
Prep time: 15 minutes
Cooking time: 5-6 hours

for the antipasti board
12 slices prosciutto di Parma
6 slices prosciutto cotto
6 slices Milano salami
6 slices finocchiona fennel salami
6 slices bresaola
200g mozzarella balls and sundried tomatoes
145g cream cheese stuffed peppers
140g Nocellara olives
120g Parmigiano Reggiano, *broken into small rough pieces*
385g piece of focaccia
1 tbsp extra virgin olive oil

for the garnish
100g wild rocket, washed
1 tbsp extra virgin olive oil
10g Parmigiano Reggiano

Feijoada is a classic dish originating from Portuguese-speaking countries but most well-known as one of the staple dishes in most Brazilian churrasco restaurants. This recipe uses chorizo sausages, smoked dry-cured bacon and cured ham hock, cooked with spices, vegetables and beans to create a one-pot flavour explosion that provides a balanced dish which is high in fibre.

FEIJOADA SAUSAGE STEW

To cook the stew, place the bacon, onion, garlic, bay leaves, carrots, celery and paprika into a large saucepan with the olive oil and fry over a medium heat until the vegetables are starting to brown and the onions are translucent. Add the chicken stock and diced fresh tomatoes and continue cooking to reduce the liquid by a third. When reduced add the tinned tomatoes and beans. Meanwhile, in a frying pan over a medium-to-high heat sear the chorizo sausages to colour on all sides and then add to the stew along with the ham hock. Cook for a further 5-10 minutes and season to taste.

To serve, portion out the stew into 6 bowls and sprinkle with fresh chopped parsley to garnish.

Nutritional information

Amount per serving	
Protein	52.4g
Fat	45.4g
Carbohydrates	42.4g
Fibre	13.2g
Energy	768kcal

Serves: 6
Prep time: 25 minutes
Cooking time: 35 minutes

for the stew
200g diced smoked bacon lardons
1 onion, *diced*
3 medium-sized garlic cloves, *peeled and finely chopped*
2-3 bay leaves
2 small carrots, *peeled and diced*
3 celery sticks, *diced*
2 tbsps smoked sweet paprika
1 tbsp extra virgin olive oil
500ml chicken stock
400g plum tomatoes, *skinned and de-seeded, diced*
400g tinned chopped tomatoes
2 tins of black beans, *drained and rinsed*
1 tin of kidney beans, *drained and rinsed*
12 fresh chorizo sausages
350g pulled ham hock

to garnish
10g parsley leaves, *finely chopped*

This recipe is quick to cook on the BBQ and tastes amazing; the char and smoke flavour take the chicken to the next level. The smoked garlic in the pesto also adds a lovely smokiness to the sauce to finish off this quick Italian dish.

GRILLED BBQ CHICKEN WITH CHARRED VEGETABLES, NEW POTATOES AND SMOKED GARLIC PESTO

For the chicken, set up the BBQ, see page 174, for direct heat cooking. Butterfly the breasts: slice lengthways, leaving a 'hinge' and try to keep both 'wings' an even thickness. Brush the chicken with the olive oil and season well with sea salt and cracked black pepper. Place on the BBQ, turning every 2 minutes until nicely charred and fully cooked all the way through. This should take 12-16 minutes depending on the temperature of the coals. Use a meat thermometer to check the core temperature is at least 72°C.

For the grilled vegetables, put the broccoli, fennel, peppers, dill and olive oil in a bowl and season with the sea salt and cracked black pepper. Toss the vegetables to fully coat them then carefully pour out onto your grilling bars on the BBQ. Turn the vegetables every minute until golden brown and tender. Put the cherry tomatoes into the bowl that had the vegetables in and toss in the leftover oil and seasoning. When the broccoli and fennel are nearly cooked, add the tomatoes. Remove the tomatoes when the skins start to split.

Chef's tip: if the grilling bars on your BBQ are quite wide you can place a wire cooling/baking rack on top.

For the potatoes, place the potatoes in a pan of water over a medium heat and bring to the boil. Simmer for 10 minutes until tender and drain. Place the potatoes in a bowl and toss with the olive oil and fennel seeds and season well. When ready to serve place the potatoes on the BBQ directly over the coals to char for 5-10 minutes, turning every minute until golden brown.

For the smoked garlic pesto, place all the ingredients into a blender and blend on a high speed until smooth and well mixed. Taste and season more if required.

To serve, on a plate or large sharing board place a bed of the vegetables followed by the chicken and garnish with the pesto, Parmigiano Reggiano, basil leaves, toasted pine nuts and finally some finely grated lemon zest.

Nutritional information

Amount per serving	
Protein	51.9g
Fat	46.6g
Carbohydrates	22.1g
Fibre	8.3g
Energy	700kcal

Serves: 4
Prep time: 30 minutes
Cooking time: 25 minutes

for the chicken
4 small chicken breasts
1 tsp extra virgin olive oil
sea salt and cracked black pepper

for the grilled vegetables
300g stem broccoli
300g fennel, *sliced into large pieces*
2 yellow peppers, *cut into large pieces*
5g fresh dill, *roughly chopped*
1 tbsp extra virgin olive oil
sea salt and cracked black pepper
270g cherry tomatoes on the vine

for the potatoes
400g new potatoes
1 tbsp extra virgin olive oil
1 tbsp fennel seeds
sea salt and cracked black pepper

for the smoked garlic pesto
60g basil, *leaves and stems*
30g Parmigiano Reggiano, *finely grated*
30g pine nuts, *toasted*
8 smoked garlic cloves, *peeled*
100ml extra virgin olive oil
sea salt and cracked black pepper

for the garnish
50g Parmigiano Reggiano, *finely grated*
10g fresh basil leaves
20g pine nuts, *toasted*
zest of 1 lemon

Harissa originated in Tunisia but is now more widely used in north African cooking. It's a spicy paste of roasted red peppers, chillies, cumin, coriander, caraway seeds, lemon and garlic which is great for marinating most meats, fish or vegetables. In this recipe, it's used to marinate a spatchcocked chicken which is then served with one of the best dips of all time – baba ghanoush, made by charring aubergines, still in their skins, over fire, giving the most amazing smoky flavour.

HARISSA ROAST CHICKEN, COUSCOUS, BABA GHANOUSH AND ROASTED SPICED CAULIFLOWER

Nutritional information

Amount per serving	
Protein	67.2g
Fat	50.5g
Carbohydrates	51.9g
Fibre	9.8g
Energy	911kcal

Serves: 4
Prep time: 30 minutes,
plus up to 24 hours marinating time
Cooking time: 60 minutes

for the chicken
1.6kg medium whole chicken
100g Greek yoghurt
juice of 1 lemon
100g harissa
sea salt and cracked black pepper

for the cauliflower
1 large cauliflower, *green leaves removed*
3 tbsps extra virgin olive oil
sea salt and cracked black pepper
35g zaatar

for the baba ghanoush
2 aubergines
4 tbsps tahini
juice of 1 lemon
1 garlic clove, peeled
1 tsp sumac
2 tbsps extra virgin olive oil

for the couscous
380g chicken stock
250g couscous
10g fresh parsley
10g fresh coriander
juice of ½ a lemon

for the garnish
1tbsp extra virgin olive oil
100g pomegranate seeds
10g chopped coriander

For the chicken and cauliflower, spatchcock the chicken: cut along one side around 1cm off the centre of the backbone from the tail to the neck with strong scissors. Then do the same on the other side, effectively removing the backbone completely. Flip the chicken over, then press down firmly on the breast with both hands to flatten it out. You should hear a slight crack as the breastbone breaks and the chicken flattens. Place the chicken on a lined baking tray. Mix the Greek yoghurt, lemon juice, harissa, salt and pepper together and rub all over the chicken. Leave to marinate for at least 2 hours or preferably overnight.

Preheat the oven to 200°C/400°F/gas mark 6. Drizzle the cauliflower with the extra virgin olive oil, season heavily with salt and pepper and place onto a lined baking tray. Place the chicken and the cauliflower into the oven for 50 minutes. Remove from the oven and baste the cauliflower with the juices in the bottom of the tray and sprinkle with the zaatar. Use a meat thermometer to check that the temperature in the thickest parts of the chicken has reached 75°C.

For the baba ghanoush, place the aubergines over the naked flame of a gas hob until they are charred heavily all over. Place in a bowl and cover with foil or cling film tightly to steam in their own heat for 10 minutes. Once cool, remove the blackened skin and discard. Place the flesh into a blender along with the tahini, lemon juice, garlic, sumac and oil and blend until smooth.

For the couscous, put the chicken stock in a pan over a high heat and bring to the boil. Pour the stock over the couscous in a heatproof bowl and cover for 15 minutes. Fluff the couscous with a fork, then add the parsley, coriander and lemon juice and mix well.

To serve, allow the chicken to rest for at least 10 minutes, then place it on a board and drizzle any juices from the bottom of the tray over. Put the cauliflower, the baba ghanoush and couscous into bowls, then drizzle with the olive oil. Garnish with the pomegranate seeds and chopped coriander. Place in the centre of the table for everyone to help themselves.

The origins of ras el hanout can be traced back to the Middle Ages. Morocco was a major spice port that linked Africa to Europe, so spices from all over the world came together there. The original blend remains unknown, but was a reflection of fine Moroccan gastronomy and found mainly in royal cities. It's a complex spice offering layers of flavour that blend earthy, spicy, sweet and bitter notes. Spice merchants would create blends of their finest spices and call them ras el hanout, which means 'head of the shop'.

HONEY AND RAS EL HANOUT BBQ CHICKEN WITH POMEGRANATE SALAD AND MINT YOGURT

Nutritional information

Amount per serving	
Protein	56.3g
Fat	51.6g
Carbohydrates	58.7g
Fibre	7.5g
Energy	910kcal

Serves: 4
Prep time: 20 minutes,
plus up to 24 hours marinating time
Cooking time: 35 minutes

for the chicken
4 garlic cloves, *peeled and grated*
5 thyme sprigs
2 tbsps olive oil
2 tbsps ras el hanout
1 tbsp harissa
1 tbsp honey
sea salt and cracked black pepper
8 skin-on, bone-in chicken thighs

for the pomegranate salad
150g giant couscous
250g frozen peas
100g cherry tomatoes
½ red onion, *peeled*
200g pomegranate seeds
1 tbsp olive oil
1 tbsp pomegranate molasses
10g parsley leaves

for the mint yogurt
160ml Greek yogurt
20g tahini
juice and zest of ½ lemon
10g fresh mint

to garnish
1 bag lamb's lettuce
1 tsp extra virgin olive oil
sea salt and cracked black pepper

For the chicken, put the garlic, thyme, olive oil, ras el hanout, harissa, honey and a generous pinch of sea salt and cracked black pepper into a large bowl. Add the chicken and mix to thoroughly coat. Leave for at least two hours or, ideally, overnight.

For the pomegranate salad, bring a medium saucepan of salted water to the boil and add the giant couscous. Cook for 10-12 minutes until tender, remove from the heat, strain and add the frozen peas. Mix thoroughly and leave for 3 minutes before rinsing in cold water to cool.

Halve the cherry tomatoes and thinly slice the red onion, add to a large bowl along with the couscous and pomegranate seeds. Pour over the olive oil and pomegranate molasses and stir through to coat the salad. Finish by finely chopping the parsley and adding to the salad.

For the mint yogurt, combine the Greek yogurt and tahini in a bowl and add the lemon zest and juice. Finely chop the mint and stir through. Season to taste with salt and pepper.

To serve, set up your BBQ for indirect cooking, see page 173, looking for a stable 180-200°C. Place the chicken thighs on a lined baking tray and cook for 20 minutes on the opposite side to the coals. Move the chicken on the rack directly above the coals to colour and char for another 10 minutes, turning regularly so that they do not colour too quickly. Check the centre of the thighs with a meat thermometer to ensure you've reached 85°C. Place back on the tray, cover with foil and rest for 5 minutes. Place some lamb's lettuce on the bottom of the plate, top with pomegranate salad followed by the chicken thighs and finish with a drizzle of the mint yogurt and extra virgin olive oil. Season with sea salt and cracked black pepper.

Iberian paella, the traditional rice dish of Valencia, is named after the traditional frying pan which would be placed on an open fire. Stock is the key to making this amazing dish, which comprises perfectly cooked bomba rice with the wonderful flavours of green beans and chicken. Pay close attention to the method in this recipe: stirring the rice will lead to disaster! Not stirring will create soft, perfectly cooked rice in the centre and crunchy, crisp rice on the edges of the pan. Traditionally an inland dish, the alternative (paella de marisco) would use seafood instead of meat and a seafood stock instead of the chicken stock.

IBERIAN PAELLA

For the paella, place a paella pan over a medium to high heat. Add the olive oil to the pan and season well with sea salt. When the salt begins to crackle add the chicken thighs, skin side down, and fry for 5-6 minutes until golden brown. Turn over, add the mushrooms and runner beans and cook for a further 5-6 minutes until everything is well caramelised. Reduce the heat to medium before adding the garlic, smoked paprika, grated tomatoes and saffron. Stir to combine. Add the rice and the stock and gently shake the pan to ensure both are well distributed and the rice is just submerged – it's important not to stir the paella from now on. Bring to a gentle simmer and allow to cook for 10 minutes, rotating the pan clockwise one quarter turn halfway through to ensure even cooking. After another 10 minutes rotate the pan again then reduce the heat to low. Place the rosemary sprigs on top and loosely cover the pan with foil. Cook for a further 10 minutes rotating the pan clockwise again one quarter halfway through. Turn off the heat but leave the paella covered for a further 10 minutes.

To serve, divide the paella between 4 plates and serve with a wedge of lemon on the side for each person.

Nutritional information

Amount per serving	
Protein	35.2g
Fat	27.5g
Carbohydrates	60.0g
Fibre	4.5g
Energy	621kcal

Serves: 4
Prep time: 20 minutes
Cooking time: 50 minutes

for the paella
2 tbsps olive oil
sea salt to taste
4 chicken thighs, bone-in, skin on, approximately 600g
100g wild mushrooms
200g runner beans, *sliced into 1-inch lengths*
3 cloves garlic, *peeled and finely chopped*
1 tbsp smoked paprika
4 vine tomatoes, *grated*
0.5g saffron
250g bomba rice
500ml chicken stock
2 sprigs of rosemary

to serve
4 lemon wedges

The tortilla or omelette could stake a claim to be the national dish of Spain: along with paella, it's eaten in all regions of the country. It's a simple dish based around eggs, potatoes and onions which makes it a fantastic base to add other ingredients and flavours to. We're keeping it authentic with three wonderful Spanish ingredients; Ibérico cheese, Serrano ham and chorizo.

IBÉRICO CHEESE TORTILLA WITH CHORIZO, SERRANO HAM, SPANISH BAKED BEANS AND WILD ROCKET

Nutritional information

Amount per serving	
Protein	42.5g
Fat	34.8g
Carbohydrates	48.4g
Fibre	11.6g
Energy	651kcal

Serves: 6
Prep time: 10 minutes
Cooking time: 40 minutes

for the tortilla
2 tbsp vegetable oil
1 medium onion, *peeled and diced*
350g potatoes, *peeled and diced*
2 cloves of garlic, *peeled and finely chopped*
2 tsps fresh thyme, *leaves only*
90g fresh baby spinach
8 large eggs
250ml semi-skimmed milk
60ml single cream
140g thinly sliced oil-packed sun-dried tomatoes
60g grated Ibérico cheese
¼ tsp sea salt
½ tsp cracked black pepper

for the Spanish baked beans
1 tsp extra virgin olive oil
2 garlic cloves, *peeled and finely diced*
250g cherry tomatoes, *halved*
1 tbsp smoked paprika
400g butter beans, *drained and rinsed*
sea salt and cracked black pepper

for the garnish
80g sliced Ibérico bellota chorizo
80g Serrano ham
50g wild rocket, *washed*
10g Manchego cheese, *finely grated*

For the tortilla, preheat the oven to 200°C/400°F/gas mark 6. Heat a 10-inch cast iron pan over a medium-to-high heat and add the vegetable oil. Add the onion and diced potato and sauté for about 4-6 minutes until lightly browned and tender, stirring occasionally. Add the garlic and fresh thyme and sauté for an additional minute. Add the spinach and sauté until just wilted. Turn off heat and evenly spread the mixture out in the pan. In a large bowl, whisk together the eggs, milk, cream, sun-dried tomatoes, Ibérico cheese, salt and pepper until just combined. Pour the egg mixture into the pan. Transfer to the oven and cook for 30-35 minutes, until the eggs are just cooked through. Finally, place the tortilla under a medium-hot grill for 1-2 minutes for a browned and crisp finish.

For the Spanish baked beans, place a frying pan on a medium heat, add the olive oil and garlic and fry for 30 seconds until starting to colour. Add the halved cherry tomatoes, smoked paprika and butter beans and cook for 5 minutes, stirring occasionally. Season with salt and pepper to taste.

To serve, let the tortilla cool for a few minutes, then top with the chorizo, Serrano ham, rocket and finely grated Manchego cheese, then slice into wedges and serve with a large spoonful of the Spanish baked beans.

The famous black-footed Iberian pig can be traced back to the Neolithic period around 12,000 years ago. Iberian pigs live in the Dehesa oak forests where they feast on acorns, which deliver their distinctive fat, high in oleic acid. This recipe uses the presa cut, a highly marbled cut from the shoulder with a distinctive nutty flavour to the meat. Ibérico pork is best eaten blushed; when properly cooked, rested and sliced, it will melt in your mouth.

IBÉRICO PORK PRESA WITH MOJO ROJO SAUCE, PATATAS BRAVAS AND CHARRED BROCCOLI

For the patatas bravas, place a large baking tray in the oven at 220°C/425°F/gas mark 7. Add the potatoes to a pan of salted water, bring to the boil over a high heat and boil for 1 minute then drain. Return the potatoes to the pan and add half a tablespoon of olive oil and salt and pepper, stirring to make sure the potatoes are fully coated. Put them into the hot baking tray, arranging them in a single layer. Return to the oven and bake for 30 minutes, turning after 15 minutes, until golden and crispy. Meanwhile, make the sauce: heat a teaspoon of olive oil in a sauté pan over a medium heat. Add the onion and sauté until soft and golden - about 8 minutes. Add the garlic and stir for 30 seconds. Add the tomatoes, paprika, cayenne pepper, Tabasco and salt, stir to combine and bring to a simmer. Reduce the heat to low and simmer for about 20 minutes, stirring occasionally. Taste and adjust seasoning if needed. Transfer to a food processor and blend to a smooth purée.

For the garlic aioli, add the mayonnaise, lemon juice and garlic to a bowl and stir to combine.

For the mojo rojo sauce, preheat the oven to 200°C/400°F/gas mark 6. Put the bell pepper and garlic on a baking tray, drizzle with olive oil and roast for 20 minutes, giving them a half-turn midway through. Once cooked leave to cool to room temperature, de-seed the pepper and remove the skin from the garlic. Place the cooked, de-seeded red pepper and garlic with all the other ingredients into a blender and pulse until well blended and smooth. Add more salt to taste.

For the Ibérico presa, season the meat with salt and cracked black pepper. Place a frying pan over a medium to high heat. Add the sunflower oil then the presa steaks and cook for 3 minutes on each side to achieve a golden-brown crust whilst retaining the blush of this incredible meat, this will be medium rare and the best way to eat this cut of pork. Transfer the steaks to a warm plate and cover with foil to rest for 2 minutes.

For the broccoli, place the broccoli on a baking tray, sprinkle with the smoked paprika, drizzle with the olive oil and toss to coat. Season with salt and cracked black pepper. Place into the oven at 200°C/400°F/gas mark 6 for 8 minutes. Serve immediately.

To serve, place the patatas bravas on the plate and drizzle with aioli. Serve the broccoli on a dish with some sea salt and cracked black pepper. On a separate plate, place the presa steaks on top of a layer of mojo rojo sauce and garnish with the flat leaf parsley.

Nutritional information

Amount per serving	
Protein	32.3g
Fat	55.1g
Carbohydrates	49.8g
Fibre	9.4g
Energy	808kcal

Serves: 2
Prep time: 30 minutes
Cooking time: 30 minutes

for the patatas bravas
250g Yukon gold potatoes, *cut into 1½cm dice*
½ tbsp olive oil
sea salt and cracked black pepper
1 tsp olive oil
1 small white onion, *peeled and diced*
2 garlic cloves, *peeled and minced*
200g tinned chopped tomatoes
1 tsp smoked paprika
¼ teaspoon cayenne pepper
2-3 dashes Tabasco sauce, *to taste*
sea salt

for the garlic aioli
40g mayonnaise
1 tsp fresh lemon juice
1 garlic clove, *peeled and grated*

for the mojo rojo
1 large red bell pepper
2 cloves garlic, *skin on*
1 tbsp olive oil
½ red chilli, *seeds removed*
½ slice white bread
1 tsp paprika
¼ tsp ground cumin
1 tbsp red wine vinegar
1½ tsps sea salt

for the Ibérico presa
240g Ibérico pork presa
sea salt and cracked black pepper
½ tbsp sunflower oil

for the broccoli
200g stem broccoli
1 tsp smoked paprika
1 tsp extra virgin olive oil
sea salt and cracked black pepper

for the garnish
10g flat leaf parsley, *roughly chopped*

This simple dish is tasty and nutritious and a quick and easy way of getting protein at breakfast. The Ibérico ham provides protein, but the fat is also high in oleic acid, a monounsaturated fatty acid which increases good (HDL) cholesterol and reduces bad (LDL) cholesterol. The fibre boost from the tomatoes and spinach complete the nutritional profile and the sourdough bread is a satiating source of healthy carbohydrates.

JAMÓN IBÉRICO AND SCRAMBLED EGGS

Nutritional information

Amount per serving	
Protein	44.8g
Fat	44.1g
Carbohydrates	44.3g
Fibre	8g
Energy	763kcal

Serves: 2
Prep time: 5 minutes
Cooking time: 5 minutes

for the spinach and tomatoes
20g unsalted butter
100g cherry tomatoes, *stalk removed and sliced in half*
140g fresh baby spinach, *washed*
sea salt and cracked black pepper

for the scrambled eggs
6 free range eggs
10g butter
sea salt and cracked black pepper

for the garnish
60g Jamón Ibérico
4 slices of seeded rye soughdough bread
10g unsalted butter
5g fresh parsley

To cook in the pan:

For the spinach and tomatoes, place a frying pan over a medium-to-high heat, add the butter and halved tomatoes and cook for 1 minute, stirring occasionally. Add the spinach, season with salt and pepper and cook for another 1-2 minutes until the spinach has wilted. Set aside.

For the scrambled eggs, place another frying pan over a medium heat and add the butter. Crack the eggs into a bowl and whisk together. Add the egg mixture to the pan and stir constantly to ensure it doesn't stick to the bottom of the pan. The perfect eggs should still be a little creamy and not dry and rubbery, this should take around 1 minute to cook. Season with sea salt and cracked black pepper.

To cook in the microwave:

For the spinach and tomatoes, place the spinach, cherry tomatoes and butter in a microwaveable bowl, then season with sea salt and cracked black pepper. Cover the bowl tightly with cling film and place in the microwave for one minute. Carefully remove the bowl and stir, then return to the microwave for another 30 seconds. The spinach should be nicely wilted and piping hot. Set aside.

For the scrambled eggs, crack the eggs into a microwaveable bowl and whisk together. Add the butter then place in the microwave for 1 minute. Remove the bowl and mix the eggs again. Season with sea salt and cracked black pepper and return to the microwave for another 30 seconds. Check the eggs again and mix: they should be creamy and not dry and rubbery.

To serve, (for both cooking methods) arrange the Jamón Ibérico on one side of a plate. Toast the sourdough, then spread lightly with unsalted butter and add to the plate. Drain any excess liquid from the spinach then top the toast with the creamy scrambled eggs, finally adding a spoonful of spinach and tomatoes. Finish with freshly ground black pepper.

Niçoise salad is great with either tuna or chicken alongside potatoes, green beans, olives and greens, making it well balanced nutritionally. This recipe uses chicken cooked in the air fryer, so it's quick and easy to prepare.

NIÇOISE SALAD WITH AIR FRYER BUTTERFLY CHICKEN

For the chicken, butterfly the breasts: slice lengthways, leaving a 'hinge' and try to keep both 'wings' an even thickness. Make the marinade: grate the garlic cloves into a large bowl, add the oil, fennel seeds, whole thyme sprigs, salt and pepper. Place the chicken into the marinade and make sure it's fully coated. Cover with cling film and place in the fridge for at least 30 minutes.

For the salad, cut the new potatoes in half, place into a saucepan and cover with water. Season well with salt, bring to a simmer and cook for 8-10 minutes until tender. Drain and set aside to cool. Trim the French beans and blanch for 2-3 minutes in boiling salted water, drain and refresh under running cold water to stop them cooking further. Remove the root and separate the leaves of the gem lettuces and wash with cold water. Thinly slice the red onion, halve the olives and tomatoes and add to a large mixing bowl along with the potatoes and beans. Add the dressing and mix well to ensure everything is coated.

For the dressing, put the mustard and vinegar into a medium mixing bowl and whisk together while slowly adding the oil. Once mixed, add the herbs, lemon juice and zest. Season to taste with sea salt and cracked black pepper.

For the eggs, bring a saucepan of water to the boil, reduce to a simmer and gently add the eggs. Cook for 7 minutes. Place the pan in the sink and run cold water over the eggs to cool them down. Peel the eggs and cut into halves.

To cook the chicken, preheat an air fryer to 220°C, place the chicken in and cook for 12-15 minutes until thoroughly cooked. Check with a food thermometer that the thickest part of the chicken has reached 72°C. Remove and rest for 3-4 minutes before serving.

To serve, arrange the lettuce leaves on the plates. Divide the dressed salad between the plates and add the eggs, lemons and the chicken, pouring any cooking juices over at the end. Season with a squeeze of fresh lemon.

Nutritional information

Amount per serving	
Protein	48.7g
Fat	32.0g
Carbohydrates	34.9g
Fibre	8.9g
Energy	604kcal

Serves: 4
Prep time: 20 minutes,
plus 30 minutes marinating time
Cooking time: 20 minutes

for the chicken
4 small chicken breasts
2 garlic cloves, *peeled and grated*
2 tbsps extra virgin olive oil
1 tsp fennel seeds
4 thyme sprigs
sea salt and cracked black pepper

for the salad
500g new potatoes
salt
200g French beans
2 gem lettuces
½ red onion
150g pitted Kalamata olives
300g vine tomatoes

for the dressing
1 tbsp Dijon mustard
1 tbsp white wine vinegar
4 tbsps extra virgin olive oil
10g chives, *finely chopped*
10g parsley, *finely chopped*
10g tarragon, *finely chopped*
zest and juice of 1 lemon
sea salt and cracked black pepper

for the eggs
2 large free-range eggs

for the garnish
2 lemons, *halved*

A tweak on ragù using pork mince to give a more mellow flavour and a softer more succulent dish. The key to any good ragù is to cook slowly and let the flavours develop whilst slowly reducing the sauce. Using fresh pasta takes this dish to the next level: the fresh bronze die fusilli gigante pasta traps the ragù in its folds. Aged Parmigiano Reggiano finishes this dish perfectly.

PORK RAGÙ WITH FRESH BRONZE DIE FUSILLI GIGANTE PASTA

For the pork ragù, in a large pan on a medium-to-high heat add the bacon, onion, carrot, celery and garlic with a little extra virgin olive oil and fry until the mixture starts to brown, stirring occasionally. Add the pork mince and oregano and fry until the mince starts to brown. Add the red wine and tomato purée and mix. Add the passata, tinned tomatoes and season with salt and pepper then reduce the heat to medium so that the ragù is gently simmering. Place a lid on, but not fully closed, allowing the steam to escape. Simmer for 60-90 minutes, stirring occasionally, until the ragù has reduced and the sauce is a thicker consistency.

For the pasta, half fill a large saucepan with water and place over a high heat to come to the boil. Add some salt and olive oil to the water. Add the pasta, stir and cook for 4-5 minutes. While the pasta is cooking, in a frying pan on a medium heat cook the garlic in a little extra virgin olive oil until starting to brown. Drain the pasta and add to the garlic in the frying pan; add the basil and mix together.

To serve, add the pasta to the ragù and gently mix. Spoon into bowls, garnish with fresh basil leaves and top with grated Parmigiano Reggiano. Season with cracked black pepper and drizzle over a little extra virgin olive oil.

Nutritional information

Amount per serving	
Protein	46.5g
Fat	28.0g
Carbohydrates	53.5g
Fibre	8.3g
Energy	676kcal

Serves: 4
Prep time: 15 minutes
Cooking time: 90 minutes

for the pork ragù
6 rashers smoked dry-cured air-dried streaky bacon, *finely chopped*
1 medium onion, *peeled and finely diced*
1 small carrot, *peeled and finely diced*
1 stick celery, *finely diced*
3 garlic cloves, *peeled and finely diced*
extra virgin olive oil
500g pork mince
1 tsp dried oregano
60ml red wine
1 tbsp tomato purée
690g tomato passata
1 tin chopped Italian tomatoes
sea salt and cracked black pepper

for the pasta
sea salt
2 tbsps extra virgin olive oil
500g fresh bronze die fusilli gigante pasta
6 garlic cloves, *peeled and finely chopped*
10g fresh basil, *finely sliced*

for the garnish
20g fresh basil leaves
60g Parmigiano Reggiano, *grated*
cracked black pepper
extra virgin olive oil

Saltimbocca is a Roman recipe that dates back centuries. This recipe uses very few ingredients which combine to create an amazing flavour. Saltimbocca was traditionally made with veal but can also be made with pork, chicken or beef. Our recipe includes lean pork medallion steaks with fresh sage and salty prosciutto ham. The steaks are dipped in flour to give a crunchy layer on the outside and juicy and succulent meat on the inside.

PORK SALTIMBOCCA

For the sweet potatoes, preheat the oven to 200°C/400°F/gas mark 6. Place the sweet potatoes and onions on a baking tray, drizzle with the olive oil and mix to fully coat. Season with sea salt and cracked black pepper and place in the oven for 25 minutes, turning the vegetables over after 15 minutes. Remove the tray from the oven.

For the saltimbocca, put the pork steaks in between two pieces of cling film and use a meat mallet or rolling pin to flatten them to an even 5mm thickness. Place a sage leaf on top of each steak then wrap a slice of prosciutto around the steak. Put a large frying pan over a medium heat and add the sunflower oil. Mix the flour and black pepper in a bowl then put the wrapped steaks into the flour making sure both sides are covered. Add the steaks to the frying pan and cook for 3 minutes on each side until golden brown. Remove from the pan and rest for 5 minutes before serving.

For the green beans, place a frying pan over a medium heat, add the olive oil, garlic, chilli and fennel seeds and fry for 1 minute, stirring constantly. Add the French beans and cook for another 2 minutes, stirring occasionally. Add the tomatoes and butter and cook for another 2 minutes until the tomatoes start to soften. Season with sea salt and cracked black pepper.

To serve, in a frying pan over a medium to high heat add the vegetable oil, leave for one minute to get hot then drop in the sage leaves to fry for 20 seconds on each side. Remove and place onto kitchen roll to absorb any excess oil. Sprinkle with salt. On each plate place some sweet potatoes, French beans and one of the pork saltimbocca. Garnish with parsley, a lemon quarter and a fried sage leaf.

Nutritional information

Amount per serving	
Protein	37.2g
Fat	37.5g
Carbohydrates	53.5g
Fibre	9.5g
Energy	525kcal

Serves: 4
Prep time: 20 minutes
Cooking time: 30 minutes

for the sweet potatoes
400g sweet potatoes, *peeled and cut into 2cm squares*
1 large red onion, *peeled and cut into 2cm pieces*
1 tbsp extra virgin olive oil
sea salt and cracked black pepper

for the saltimbocca
4 pork loin medallion steaks
4 large sage leaves
4 slices prosciutto
1 tbsp sunflower oil
40g plain flour
cracked black pepper

for the green beans
1 tsp extra virgin olive oil
4 cloves of garlic, *peeled and finely sliced*
1 red chilli, *de-seeded and finely chopped*
½ tsp fennel seeds
320g French beans, *topped and tailed*
200g cherry tomatoes, *stalks removed, cut in half*
20g unsalted butter
sea salt and cracked black pepper

for the garnish
2 tbsps vegetable oil
4 sage leaves
sea salt
10g fresh parsley, *chopped*
1 lemon, *quartered*

The star of the show here is not the lamb, but the houmous. Houmous is a Middle Eastern food claimed by all and owned by none, but likely Egyptian in origin. This dish was made famous by Yotam Ottolenghi in his book Jerusalem. It's a show-stopping centrepiece made for sharing and uses houmous as its base, not just as a dip. The ingredients are all winners in their own right, but it's the houmous that links them together and turns them into an amazing flavour combination.

ROAST LEG OF LAMB WITH WHIPPED FETA, FLATBREADS, TOMATO AND APRICOT SALAD, AND HOUMOUS

For the lamb, combine the spices, olive oil, garlic, salt and pepper into a paste and rub all over the lamb. Leave to marinate for at least 2 hours, or ideally overnight. Preheat the oven to 180°C/350°F/gas mark 4 and place the lamb in to roast for 45 minutes, or until an internal temperature of 60°C is reached on a meat thermometer for medium rare lamb, or 70°C for medium/well done. Take the lamb out of the oven and rest it, covered in foil, for 20 minutes.

For the whipped feta, blend the feta, Greek yoghurt, lemon juice and olive oil in a food processor until smooth. Fold in the chopped mint and place in a bowl. Cover and store in the fridge.

For the flatbreads, mix the plain flour, salt and black pepper and slowly add the warm water, mixing until it comes together. Add the olive oil and knead until you have a soft dough. Leave to stand in the bowl covered in a damp tea towel for 30 minutes. Divide the dough into 8 balls, flatten them and dry fry on both sides in a pan over a high heat until puffed up. Set aside wrapped in foil until the lamb is ready.

For the salad, stone and quarter the apricots. Slice the tomatoes in half and mix with the apricots in a large bowl. Sprinkle with the sumac and mix. Add the remaining ingredients and mix.

To serve, carve the lamb and serve on a board surrounded by the warm flatbreads. Arrange the tomato and apricot salad, whipped feta and houmous in serving bowls.

Nutritional information

Amount per serving	
Protein	51.6g
Fat	55.6g
Carbohydrates	44.5g
Fibre	6.2g
Energy	873kcal

Serves: 8
Prep time: 20 minutes,
plus up to 24 hours marinating time
Cooking time: 65 minutes

for the lamb
1 tsp ground cumin
1 tsp ground coriander
1 tsp paprika
1 tsp turmeric
2 tbsps extra virgin olive oil
4 garlic cloves, *peeled and grated*
sea salt and cracked black pepper
1.2kg bone-in leg of lamb

for the whipped feta
400g feta
3 tbsps Greek yoghurt
juice of half a lemon
3 tbsps extra virgin olive oil
5g fresh mint leaves, *chopped*

for the flatbreads
250g plain flour
sea salt and cracked black pepper
125ml warm water, *about body temperature*
3 tbsps extra virgin olive oil

for the salad
420g fresh apricots
400g cherry tomatoes
1 tsp sumac
2 tbsps pomegranate molasses
1 tbsp extra virgin olive oil
80g pomegranate seeds
5g fresh parsley leaves, *chopped*

to serve
400g RAMONA'S houmous
15g fresh coriander, *chopped*

Shakshuka is a Tunisian dish that has variations all over the middle east. This dish is perfect as a weekend breakfast or brunch. The chicken adds protein so it feels substantial and it's packed full of flavours and textures, so it's really tasty, but it is also nutritionally balanced and a great source of fibre.

SHAKSHUKA WITH CHICKEN, FETA AND SPICED CRISPY CHICKPEAS

Nutritional information

Amount per serving	
Protein	33.3g
Fat	38.8g
Carbohydrates	44.3g
Fibre	11.7g
Energy	641kcal

Serves: 4
Prep time: 10 minutes,
plus up to 2 hours marinating time
Cooking time: 60 minutes

for the chicken
300g chicken thighs, boneless and skinless, *diced small*
50g harissa paste

for the tomato sauce
1 tbsp extra virgin olive oil
1 large red onion, *peeled and finely diced*
2 cloves of garlic, *peeled and finely chopped*
1 red chilli, *seeds removed and finely chopped*
400g chopped tinned tomatoes
400g cherry tomatoes, *halved*
1 tbsp honey
sea salt and cracked black pepper
1 red pepper, *seeds removed and thinly sliced*
1 yellow pepper, *seeds removed and thinly sliced*
50g feta, *crumbled*
4 large free-range eggs

for the crispy chickpeas
300g chickpeas, *drained and rinsed*
1 tbsp extra virgin olive oil
20g harissa paste
1 tsp garlic granules
sea salt and cracked black pepper

for the garnish
10g coriander leaves
zest of half a lemon
sea salt and cracked black pepper

For the chicken, put the diced chicken and harissa paste into a bowl and mix until the chicken is well coated. Cover with cling film and put in the fridge to marinate for at least 20 minutes and up to two hours.

For the tomato sauce, place a large frying pan on a medium heat and add the oil. When hot add the marinated chicken, onion, garlic and chilli and cook for 4 minutes, turning occasionally to brown the meat. Add the tinned tomatoes, halved cherry tomatoes and honey and season with sea salt and cracked black pepper. Reduce the heat to low and simmer for 25 minutes stirring occasionally so the sauce doesn't burn. Add the peppers and cook for another 5 minutes. Sprinkle on the feta cheese and crack 4 eggs on the top of the tomato mixture. Place a lid on the pan and simmer for a further 5-10 minutes until the eggs are cooked to your liking.

For the crispy chickpeas, preheat the oven to 180°C/350°F/gas mark 4. Put the chickpeas in a bowl with the olive oil, harissa paste and garlic granules and season with salt and pepper. Mix together then pour into a baking tray and place in the oven for 20 minutes, mixing well halfway through. Roast until crisp.

To serve, sprinkle the chickpeas on top of the shakshuka and garnish with the coriander and finely grated lemon zest. Season with sea salt and cracked black pepper.

Bratwurst, kartoffelsalat, sauerkraut and sweet mustard – *German*

Grilled mici pork rolls with cucumber and dill salad – *Romanian*

Pork bigos stew – *Polish*

Pork goulash with potato dumplings – *Hungarian*

Pork kibinai with beetroot and red cabbage slaw – *Lithuanian*

NORTHWEST AND EASTERN EUROPEAN

Traditional ***Northwest and Easter***
and hearty dishes of meat and ro
foods which provide a complete sour
unprocessed ingredients. Their mai
meats such as veal, beef and mutto
– typically nutritionally dense food
energy and to provid

uropean cuisines feature substantial
getables, creating smoky comfort
vital nutrients made with whole and
gredients are chicken, pork and red
ften with dumplings and pastries
nerally high in salt and fat for
armth in cold winters

Bratwurst is perhaps the most famous of Germany's many sausages, served at festivals and feasts. Recipes for this iconic sausage vary by region as with so many cultural favourites. They are generally made from minced pork and/or veal, seasoned with herbs and spices such as nutmeg, coriander and ginger. We've kept it traditional, serving them with a simple potato salad and sauerkraut which makes a wonderfully tangy accompaniment to the bratwurst.

BRATWURST, KARTOFFELSALAT, SAUERKRAUT AND SWEET MUSTARD

Nutritional information

Amount per serving	
Protein	27.7g
Fat	57.0g
Carbohydrates	33.4g
Fibre	7.2g
Energy	765kcal

Serves: 4
Prep time: 15 minutes
Cooking time: 60 minutes

for the kartoffelsalat
600g yellow waxy potatoes, *washed*
180g curly kale, *finely chopped*
1 small red onion, *peeled and cut into large pieces*
1 tsp sweet yellow mustard
2 tbsps white wine vinegar
sea salt and cracked black pepper
100ml beef stock

for the bratwurst
8 bratwurst sausages
1 tbsp sunflower oil

for the garnish
360g sauerkraut
sweet yellow mustard
10g fresh parsley
sea salt and cracked black pepper

For the kartoffelsalat, place the potatoes in a pan filled with cold water and season well with sea salt. Place over a medium heat, bring to the boil and simmer gently for 10 minutes. Add the kale and cook for another 5 minutes. Drain and allow to cool to room temperature. Peel and slice the potatoes then place them in a bowl with the kale, red onion, mustard and vinegar, then mix and season with salt and pepper. Bring the beef stock to the boil and pour over the potato mix. Leave the potatoes to soak in the stock for at least 30 minutes – the longer the better for the flavour to develop.

For the bratwurst, pan fry the sausages in the oil on a low-to-medium heat for 15 to 20 minutes, turning often until golden brown on all sides.

To serve, put two bratwurst on each plate along with a large spoon of the kartoffelsalat, sauerkraut and sweet yellow mustard. Garnish with fresh parsley and season with sea salt and cracked black pepper.

This recipe is a take on pork mici rolls from Romania. It's traditionally served with bread, chips and sweet yellow mustard: we've tweaked the recipe to make it a little more nutritionally balanced with a Romanian cucumber and dill salad and some toasted, seeded sourdough bread. The mici rolls are spiced to perfection as well as being juicy on the inside and caramelised on the outside.

GRILLED MICI PORK ROLLS WITH CUCUMBER AND DILL SALAD

Nutritional information

Amount per serving	
Protein	45.5g
Fat	46.1g
Carbohydrates	32.3g
Fibre	6.2g
Energy	717kcal

Serves: 4
Prep time: 10 minutes,
plus 2 hours marinating time
Cooking time: 30 minutes

for the pork rolls
500g pork mince (20% fat)
300g beef mince (15% fat)
2 tsps paprika
4 garlic cloves, *peeled and finely diced*
50ml premium lager
½ tsp bicarbonate of soda
juice of ½ a lemon
2 tsps dried thyme
¼ tsp ground coriander
¼ tsp cumin
pinch of nutmeg
1 beef stock cube or stock pot
sea salt and cracked black pepper

for the cucumber salad
1 large cucumber, *finely sliced*
1 small red onion, *peeled and finely sliced*
2 small garlic cloves, *peeled and finely sliced*
15g dill, *finely chopped*
1 tbsp olive oil
1 tsp white wine vinegar
sea salt and cracked black pepper
220g cherry tomatoes on the vine
1 tbsp extra virgin olive oil
sea salt and cracked black pepper

to serve
4 slices of seeded sourdough bread, *toasted*
80g sweet yellow mustard
1 bag of mixed leaf lettuce

For the pork rolls, place all the ingredients in a bowl and mix, using a wooden spoon. Cover the bowl with cling film and leave for 2 hours to marinade. Shape the meat into 8 equal-sized balls and roll into log shapes. Cook in a frying pan or griddle pan with a little oil over a medium heat or on a BBQ, turning every minute until cooked thoroughly. Check with a meat thermometer that the centre of each roll has reached 72°C.

For the cucumber salad, put the cucumber, onion, garlic, dill, olive oil and white wine vinegar into a bowl and season with salt and pepper. Gently toss the cucumber to coat fully with the oil, vinegar and herbs. Heat your grill on the highest setting. Place the tomatoes on a baking tray and drizzle with the olive oil and season with salt and pepper. Place under the grill for 5 minutes until the tomatoes have softened and the skins start to split.

To serve, place the toasted sourdough on the plate and spread with a generous amount of mustard. Top with the salad leaves, then the cucumber dill salad. Add the grilled tomatoes and the pork rolls. Drizzle with a little more mustard.

Bigos is a national dish from Poland, around 700 years old. It's traditionally a provision for travellers as well as being eaten at outdoor events, such as Kulig or Polish sleigh ride. Originally made with wild game, bigos is now made with many different meats, particularly the kielbasa smoked sausage, with pork shoulder and either bacon or smoked ham hock, all stewed with sauerkraut, shredded fresh cabbage and spices. You will be amazed by the flavours in this authentic recipe. There's the earthy tones from the porcini mushrooms, salty sourness from the sauerkraut, smoke from the sausage and bacon and sweetness from the honey. Together with the spices and tender pork shoulder, it really is a wonderful combination of flavours.

PORK BIGOS STEW

For the bigos, if using dehydrated mushrooms, place them in a bowl and cover with 200ml of boiling water. Set aside for 30 minutes. Add the cabbage to a large pot and cover with the chicken stock and water. Bring to the boil then reduce heat to a minimum and simmer. Take the sauerkraut from the jar and rinse under cold water; chop roughly and add to the cabbage and stir together. Preheat a frying pan to a medium heat, add the butter and when melted, sauté the onions until soft. Add to the cabbage pot. In the same pan fry the bacon lardons and sliced kielbasa until golden brown and add to the pot. Still using the same pan, sear the pork on all sides until golden brown, then add to the pot with all the juices. Stir all well, add the chopped prunes, rehydrated mushrooms with all the liquid or the fresh mushrooms if using, tomato purée, honey, mustard and red wine. Stir well to combine. Using a pestle and mortar grind the caraway seeds, coriander seeds and juniper berries. Mix with all your remaining herbs and spices, then transfer to the pot and stir. Place a lid on top and leave to simmer for 3 hours, stirring frequently to ensure the cabbage does not burn.

To serve, cut a loaf of sourdough bread into slices, divide the stew into 6 medium-sized bowls and add the slices of bread on the side to dip into the juices. This recipe is even better when chilled after cooking and reheated the following day.

Nutritional information

Amount per serving	
Protein	43.4g
Fat	39.4g
Carbohydrates	57.6g
Fibre	13.5g
Energy	786kcal

Serves: 6
Prep time: 45 minutes
Cooking time: 3 hours

for the bigos

50g of dehydrated porcini mushrooms (or 200g of fresh porcini mushrooms), *sliced*
500g white cabbage, *finely sliced*
500ml chicken stock
200ml water
1kg jar sauerkraut
30g unsalted butter
2 medium onions, *peeled and sliced*
180g air-dried dry-cured smoked bacon lardons
300g Polish-style smoked kielbasa, *halved lengthways and sliced into 10mm slices*
300g pork shoulder, *diced*
50g prunes, *pitted and chopped roughly*
3 tbsps tomato purée
2 tbsps honey
2 tbsps Dijon mustard
200ml red wine
1 tsp caraway seeds
1 tsp coriander seeds
4 juniper berries
2 tbsps sea salt
2 tbsps cracked black pepper
4 bay leaves
1 tsp ground allspice
2 tbsps marjoram
2 tsps smoked sweet paprika
1 tsp chilli powder

to serve

12 slices of crusty white sourdough bread

Goulash is a traditional stew from Hungary. Its nomadic roots date back to the 9th century, when Magyar shepherds would simmer meats, onions and other ingredients with water before drying them in sheep's stomachs and then re-hydrating with water at mealtimes. This goulash is a real winter warmer and so easy to make. The rich and hearty combination of the slow-cooked pork, tomatoes and sweet paprika really works with the light potato dumplings.

PORK GOULASH WITH POTATO DUMPLINGS

For the goulash, place a large pan on a low-to-medium heat and melt the beef dripping for 5 minutes. Brown the pork in the pan in batches then set aside. Add the onion to the pan to sweat with a pinch of sea salt. Once softened add the peppers, pork, garlic, sweet paprika, caraway seeds and tomato paste and sweat for another 5 minutes. Add the plain flour and stir in well; cook for a further 5 minutes. Add the beef stock in 3 batches, mixing each fully before adding the next portion. Let the goulash simmer for 2 hours with the lid on.

For the potato dumplings, peel the potatoes and place them in a pot filled with water to just cover. Bring to a rolling boil over a high heat until the potatoes are cooked through. Strain and let steam dry for 15 minutes. Pass the potatoes through a ricer or sieve to get a smooth purée. Add the egg, plain flour, potato starch, nutmeg and sea salt and mix through. Form the mix into 6 even-sized balls and place on top of the goulash for the last 30 minutes of simmering.

To serve, spoon the goulash into bowls with a dumpling each, top with a spoon of sour cream and sprinkle with chopped chives.

Nutritional information

Amount per serving	
Protein	54.4g
Fat	25.3g
Carbohydrates	59.0g
Fibre	7.0g
Energy	667kcal

Serves: 6
Prep time: 15 minutes
Cooking time: 2½ hours

for the goulash
2 tbsps beef dripping
600g pork shoulder, *in large dice*
1 white onion, *peeled and sliced*
sea salt
2 red peppers, *sliced*
3 garlic cloves, *peeled and finely chopped*
1 tbsp sweet paprika
1 tsp caraway seeds
4 tbsps tomato paste
1 tbsp plain flour
600ml beef stock

for the potato dumplings
335g Maris Piper potatoes
1 small egg
110g plain flour
1½ tbsps potato starch
¼ tsp ground nutmeg
sea salt

to garnish
4 tbsps sour cream
10g chives, *thinly sliced*

Kibinai are little crescent moon-shaped pies filled with pork and vegetables. They're a popular dish, widely available in Lithuania and eaten at home or as street food. They're served hot or cold, as a main dish or a snack and they taste fantastic alongside this tangy red cabbage slaw.

PORK KIBINAI WITH BEETROOT AND RED CABBAGE SLAW

For the red slaw, mix together the vegetables and seasonings, leave to marinate for a couple of hours or overnight in the fridge, then check for seasoning and finish with the flat leaf parsley. Serve at room temperature.

For the pastry, place the flour, butter and salt in a food processor and blitz until you achieve a fine crumb. Add in the eggs and sour cream and mix until the dough comes together. Wrap the pastry in cling film and chill for a minimum of 2 hours.

For the pork filling, mix all of the ingredients gently. Set aside.

For the egg wash, crack the eggs into a bowl, season with salt and beat together until combined.

To assemble the kibinai, roll out the pastry to a 2mm thick large rectangle, cut out 8 circles 15-20cm in diameter, glaze the rim with the beaten egg and place about 120g of meat mix into the centre of each disc. Fold into a semi-circle, pushing out as much air as you can during the process. Ensure the edges are fully sealed. Stand each pastry on its folded edge and lightly squash to flatten the bases so they stand up (they should look like mini Cornish pasties!). Crimp the edges of the pastry with your thumb and forefinger, twisting as you go. Repeat along the edge of each pastry then glaze with the egg wash and chill for a minimum of 1 hour. Bake in a pre-heated oven at 160°C/325°F/gas mark 3 for 45 minutes until golden brown and crisp. Serve warm alongside the red slaw.

Nutritional information

Amount per serving	
Protein	27.4g
Fat	50.7g
Carbohydrates	75.6g
Fibre	6.0g
Energy	857kcal

Serves: 8
Prep time: 45 minutes,
plus up to 24 hours marinating time
Cooking time: 45 minutes

for the red slaw
½ large red cabbage, *finely sliced*
2 cooked whole beetroots, *peeled and grated*
1 small red onion, *peeled and finely diced*
1 apple, skin on, grated
1 tbsp grated fresh horseradish, or good quality horseradish sauce
2 tbsps rapeseed oil
1 tsp sea salt
1 tbsp cider vinegar
50ml apple juice
1 tbsp honey
10g flat leaf parsley, *roughly chopped*

for the pastry:
600g plain flour
300g unsalted butter, *diced*
2 tsps sea salt
2 eggs, *beaten*
100g sour cream

for the filling
500g minced pork
100g minced smoked bacon
1 handful of chopped fresh mixed herbs, such as sage, parsley and tarragon
1 tbsp sea salt
1 tsp dried marjoram
1 tsp mustard seeds
½ white onion, *peeled and diced*
50g white breadcrumbs
1 tsp cracked black pepper
3 tbsps sour cream
3 cloves of garlic, *peeled and finely chopped*
1 egg, beaten

for the egg wash
2 eggs
sea salt

Chicken adobo with sticky rice, pak choi and broccoli – *Filipino*

Chicken Buddha bowl with quinoa and avocado dressing – *Asian*

Chicken rendang – *Indonesian*

Crispy soy, garlic and ginger air fryer pork belly with egg fried rice and sweet and sour vegetables – *Asian*

Gochujang pork ramen – *Korean*

Katsu chicken with garlic and chilli sugar snap peas and sticky rice – *Japanese*

Miso and soy pork chop, sesame-glazed sugar snap peas and miso boulangère potatoes – *Asian*

Miso, hot honey pork and rice noodle lettuce cups – *Asian*

Pork bo ssam with sticky rice and kimchi stir fry – *Korean*

Pulled pork with pit beans and charred gochujang corn on the cob – *Korean*

Salt and chilli chicken wings with loaded new potato wedges – *Chinese*

Szechuan pork stir fry – *Chinese*

Teriyaki chicken with edamame bean and yuzu noodle salad – *Japanese*

ASIAN

This chapter explores traditional recipe
have been central to the developmen
South East Asia is known for its uniqu
like curries, stir fries and noodles. We'v
re-framed in a modern context t

rom *Asia*, where pigs and chickens
f cultures for thousands of years.
avours and ingredients including dishes
een inspired by recipes from the past,
ecognise the latest food trends

Chicken adobo is indigenous to the Philippines and is the country's most recognisable dish. The pre-colonial people of the Philippine archipelago often cooked or prepared their food with vinegar and salt to preserve it in the tropical climate. Spanish settlers invaded during the 16th century and witnessing this traditional Philippine method called it adobo, the Spanish word for marinade.

CHICKEN ADOBO WITH STICKY RICE, PAK CHOI AND BROCCOLI

For the rice, put the rinsed rice into a pan with the water and season well with salt. Put the pan over a medium-to-high heat and bring to the boil. Stir, place a lid on the pan and let the steam build up inside for 30 seconds. Turn off the heat and let the rice sit in the pan with the lid on for 15 minutes. Fluff up with a fork.

For the chicken, put a large frying pan over a medium heat, season the chicken thighs all over with salt, pepper and vegetable oil and place, skin side down, in the hot pan. Fry for 6 to 8 minutes until the skin has become golden brown, then flip over and add all the other ingredients. Bring to a simmer for 15 minutes.

For the pak choi and broccoli, place a frying pan on a high heat and add the vegetable oil. Fry the pak choi and stem broccoli for 1 minute on each side until starting to brown, but still crunchy and green. Season with sea salt and cracked black pepper.

To serve, remove the bay leaves from the chicken and serve two chicken thighs each on top of the rice. Add a half of pak choi and broccoli to each plate and spoon over some of the sauce. Sprinkle with spring onions and sliced chillies.

Nutritional information

Amount per serving	
Protein	49.9g
Fat	51.6g
Carbohydrates	50.0g
Fibre	6.6g
Energy	858kcal

Serves: 4
Prep time: 10 minutes
Cooking time: 30 minutes

for the rice

200g sushi rice, *rinsed until the water runs clear*
200ml water
sea salt

for the chicken

8 bone-in, skin-on chicken thighs
sea salt and cracked black pepper
1 tsp vegetable oil
100ml soy sauce
400ml coconut milk
100ml rice wine vinegar
2 tbsp granulated white sugar
1½ tsps cracked black pepper
8 garlic cloves, *peeled and finely chopped*
3 bay leaves
4 spring onions, *roughly chopped*

for the pak choi and broccoli

1 tsp of vegetable oil
2 heads of pak choi, *cut in half lengthways*
400g stem broccoli
sea salt and cracked black pepper

for the garnish

2 spring onions, finely sliced
1 red chilli, finely sliced

Buddha woke before dawn and carried his bowl through the streets. Local people put food into the bowl as a donation and he would eat whatever was given. Filled with wholesome offerings, the bowl reflected a time before processed foods existed and inspired the name of the dish. Our Buddha bowl is an interpretation of this story and symbolises the Buddhist ideal of balance. It brings together a harmonious mix of ingredients including tender chicken thighs, avocado, grains, quinoa, crispy chickpeas, spinach and red cabbage, creating a nourishing and wholesome meal which is high in protein and fibre.

CHICKEN BUDDHA BOWL WITH QUINOA AND AVOCADO DRESSING

For the chicken, place the chicken thighs into a bowl. Add the ras el hanout, honey, sea salt, lemon, garlic and chilli flakes and mix well.

Cover and chill for at least 3 hours, preferably overnight. Remove from the fridge 20 minutes before you start cooking. Preheat the oven to 200°C/400°F/ gas mark 6, place the thighs on a baking tray, drizzle lightly with the olive oil and roast for 35-40 minutes until charred and cooked through. Use a meat thermometer to check the chicken has reached 85°C in the thickest part.

For the crispy chickpeas, in a bowl, toss the chickpeas with the paprika, salt and oil. Transfer to a lined baking tray and cook in the oven at 200°C/400°F/ gas mark 6 for 30 minutes until crisp.

For the avocado dressing, add all the ingredients to a food blender or food processor and blitz to a smooth purée. Season with sea salt and cracked black pepper to taste.

To serve, divide the red cabbage, spinach, carrot, avocado, edamame beans, spring onions and cooked quinoa into four deep bowls. Slice the chicken thighs and place on the top. Top with the chickpeas and garnish with the avocado dressing, sriracha sauce and nigella seeds. Season with salt and pepper and serve.

Nutritional information

Amount per serving	
Protein	36.9g
Fat	20.8g
Carbohydrates	43.6g
Fibre	9.1g
Energy	510kcal

Serves: 4
Prep time: 20 minutes,
plus up to 24 hours marinating time
Cooking time: 45 minutes

for the chicken
4 boneless skinless chicken thighs
1 tbsp ras el hanout
2 tbsps runny honey
1 tsp sea salt
juice of 1 lemon
3 garlic cloves, *peeled and finely chopped*
½ tsp dried chilli flakes
1 tbsp olive oil

for the crispy chickpeas
200g tinned chickpeas, *drained, rinsed*
1 tsp smoked paprika.
½ tsp salt
1 tbsp olive oil

for the avocado dressing
1 ripe avocado, *halved, skin and stone removed*
10 g fresh parsley
10 g fresh coriander
1 tbsp lime juice
50ml water
½ tsp salt
½ tsp black pepper

for the vegetables
1 small red cabbage, *finely sliced*
100g washed baby spinach
2 carrots, *peeled and grated on the largest holes of a grater*
2 ripe avocados, *halved, skin and stone removed, and sliced*
175g edamame beans, *pre-cooked*
1 bunch spring onions, *trimmed and finely sliced*

to serve
250g cooked quinoa
60g sriracha sauce
1 tsp nigella seeds
sea salt and cracked black pepper

Rendang is one of the stand-out Asian dishes. The combination of ingredients and spices with coconut milk and toasted coconut works so well with both chicken and beef. This recipe uses chicken legs as the darker meat from the chicken is so much more flavoursome and gives better results with longer cooking times. Sweet potatoes help thicken the sauce, give another layer of sweetness to the recipe and are a good source of fibre.

CHICKEN RENDANG

To marinade the chicken, remove any excess skin from the chicken legs and remove the knuckle from the end of the chicken leg – a single sharp chop should do it. Mix all the other ingredients together in a bowl, add the chicken legs and mix well to fully coat. Marinate for 2 hours or ideally overnight.

For the spice mix, in a large frying pan, add all the spice mix ingredients and place over a medium heat. Cook for 90 seconds until the mixture starts to sizzle. Add the chicken and any juices from the marinade to the pan.

To make the rendang, pour the boiling water over the dried chillies and leave to soak for 5 minutes. In a food processor or blender, add the shallots, lemon grass, garlic, ginger, palm sugar, fish sauce, tamarind paste and chillies and blitz to a smooth paste. Then add the paste mixture to the chicken and spice mix and mix together. Remove the soaked chillies from the water and chop, then add the chillies and the water to the pan. Add the coconut milk, chicken stock and lime leaves, turn the heat to low and cook for 30 minutes, turning the chicken over every 5 minutes. Add the sweet potatoes, stir in and cook for another 15 minutes, turning the chicken every 5 minutes. Add the French beans, stir in and cook for the final 5 minutes. Season with sea salt and cracked black pepper, add the lime zest and juice and stir through.

For the jasmine rice, add the rice, coconut milk, water and toasted coconut to a pan, season well and bring to the boil over a medium heat. Stir occasionally so that the rice doesn't stick. Once boiling, place the lid on the pan, turn off the heat and leave for 15 minutes. Use a fork to fluff up the rice.

To serve, divide the rice into 4 bowls, topping each with the sweet potato and green bean rendang sauce and one chicken leg. Garnish with half a lime and some fresh coriander leaves.

Nutritional information

Amount per serving	
Protein	44.4g
Fat	58.3g
Carbohydrates	51.5g
Fibre	10.7g
Energy	889kcal

Serves: 4
Prep time: 20 minutes,
plus up to 24 hours marinating time
Cooking time: 50 minutes

for the chicken marinade
4 chicken legs
2 garlic cloves, *peeled and finely chopped*
20g ginger, *peeled and finely chopped*
½ tsp ground turmeric
1 tsp galangal root paste
1 red chilli, *seeds removed, finely chopped*
sea salt and cracked black pepper
2 tbsps water

for the spice mix
4 cardamon pods, *crushed with a knife*
1 tsp ground turmeric
1 tbsp ground cumin
1 tbsp ground coriander
2 cinnamon sticks
2 star anise
1 tbsp sunflower oil
50g desiccated coconut, *toasted*

for the rendang
80ml boiling water
4 dried Thai red chillies
2 shallots, *peeled*
3 lemon grass, *finely chopped*
6 garlic cloves, *peeled*
50g ginger, *peeled and finely chopped*
1 tbsp palm sugar
1 tbsp fish sauce
1 tbsp tamarind paste
2 red chillies, *seeds removed*
400ml coconut milk
200ml chicken stock
2 lime leaves
200g sweet potatoes, *peeled and cut into 2cm cubes*
320g French beans, *topped, tailed and cut in half*
sea salt and cracked black pepper
1 lime, *zest and juice*

for the jasmine rice
200g jasmine rice
200ml coconut milk
200ml water
20g desiccated coconut, *toasted*
sea salt and cracked black pepper

for the garnish
2 limes, *cut in half*
10g fresh coriander

This really is a modern classic. Dishes like this are trending on TikTok, bringing Asian pork belly to youth culture and fusing traditional recipes and flavours with modern quick and simple cooking. It's full of flavour and texture; crispy crackling, tender succulent pork belly and egg fried rice, with a hearty portion of fibre-rich vegetables.

CRISPY SOY, GARLIC AND GINGER AIR FRYER PORK BELLY WITH EGG FRIED RICE AND SWEET AND SOUR VEGETABLES

For the marinade, place all the ingredients in a bowl, stir and set aside.

For the pork belly, place the pork belly, rind side down, on a large chopping board. Using a sharp knife, make some diagonal cuts into the meat, going only halfway through. Spread the marinade over the meat, working it into the cuts but being careful not to get any on the rind (this would prevent it from 'crackling' properly). Place the pork, meat side down, on a piece of tin foil and wrap the foil up the sides of the belly, leaving only the top of the rind visible. Place the belly into the air fryer, brush the top of the rind with the white vinegar and coat with a thick layer of table salt. Cook at 160°C for 50 minutes. Lift the layer of baked salt off, brushing off any excess. Brush the top of the belly with the vegetable oil and sprinkle lightly with table salt. Place back into the air fryer and cook at 210°C for 30 minutes. Open the drawer slightly and allow the belly to rest in the drawer where it will stay warm for at least 20 minutes.

For the egg fried rice, put the rice, water and salt into a saucepan and place over a high heat. Stir occasionally until the water starts to boil. Place a lid on the pan and allow the heat to build up in the pan for 20 seconds then turn off the heat. Leave the rice to absorb all the water for 20 minutes, then use a fork to fluff it up. Add the vegetable oil to a wok or large frying pan over a high heat and when really hot crack in the two eggs. Quickly mix the eggs to make a scrambled egg-like mixture. Add the rice and toss with the egg until all mixed together.

For the vegetables, place a large frying pan or wok over a high heat until smoking hot. Add the oil, the garlic and all of the vegetables and stir fry for 90 seconds, tossing occasionally. Add the kecap manis and vinegar and coat the vegetables. Reserve any sauce to garnish.

To serve, on a chopping board, place the pork belly crackling side down and using a sharp knife slice into 8 equal slices. Place a portion of the egg fried rice on a plate, spoon over the vegetables and top with two slices of crispy pork belly. Garnish with thinly sliced spring onions, then pour over the remaining sauce.

Nutritional information

Amount per serving	
Protein	56.3g
Fat	45.6g
Carbohydrates	33.0g
Fibre	6.7g
Energy	782kcal

Serves: 4
Prep time: 20 minutes
Cooking time: 100 minutes

for the marinade
1 tsp white pepper
2 tsps Chinese five spice
2 garlic cloves, *peeled and finely grated*
25g ginger, *peeled and grated*
1 tsp sugar
1 tsp table salt
40g rice wine vinegar

for the pork belly
640g pork belly square, rind on
1 tsp white distilled vinegar
table salt
1 tsp vegetable oil

for the egg fried rice
240g basmati rice
460g water
1 tsp salt
1 tbsp vegetable oil
2 large free-range eggs

for the vegetables
1 tbsp vegetable oil
2 garlic cloves, *peeled and finely diced*
1 red pepper, *seeds removed and large diced*
1 yellow pepper, *seeds removed and large diced*
300g stem broccoli
1 red onion, *peeled and large diced*
100g sugar snap peas
100g kecap manis
30g rice wine vinegar

for the garnish
50g spring onion, *finely sliced*

Pork ramen is a soup-like broth with noodles: classic Japanese comfort food. We've fused it with the addition of gochugang paste, a Korean condiment made from fermented soy beans, soy sauce and chilli which delivers a powerful kick. It's a popular choice to add depth and umami flavour to dishes and it works so well against the simplicity of the ramen, topped with egg for a healthy protein hit.

GOCHUJANG PORK RAMEN

For the pork, put the water into a mixing bowl and thoroughly whisk in the white miso paste until fully dissolved. Place the shoulder steaks into the bowl, ensuring they are fully submerged. Leave to marinate for one hour or ideally overnight. Once brined, dry the steaks off with a paper towel. In a bowl mix the gochujang paste and honey, add the shoulder steaks and mix to ensure they are generously covered in the marinade. Leave to marinate for 20 minutes.

For the broth, put the soy sauce, mirin, rice wine and honey into a small bowl. Whisk thoroughly to combine and keep to one side. Put the chicken stock into a large pan over a medium heat. Add the garlic, ginger, porcini mushrooms and spring onion tops and simmer for 30 minutes. Strain the stock and put it back into the pan. Stir in the soy sauce, mirin, rice wine and honey mixture and remove from the heat.

To cook the shoulder steaks, heat a grill to medium/high and grill the steaks for 16 minutes, turning halfway through. Leave to rest for 5 minutes.

For the garnish, place a medium-sized pan of water over a high heat and bring to a rolling boil. Add the eggs and boil for 6 minutes for a runny egg or 7½ minutes for a firmer yolk. Once boiled, place straight into cold water and leave to cool. Peel the eggs and place to once side. Place a griddle pan over a medium-to-high heat. Brush the pak choi with a little sunflower oil and then place on the griddle for 3 minutes to colour, turning halfway through. When cooked remove the pak choi from the pan and reserve for later.

To serve, place the broth back on to a low heat and bring to the boil. Take 4 bowls and arrange the carrots, red cabbage, noodles and pak choi in the bowl. Ladle the desired amount of hot broth over the vegetables. Slice and add the shoulder steaks. Finish each bowl with the chillies, radish slices, half a boiled egg, sliced spring onions and a sprinkle of nigella seeds and coriander leaves.

Nutritional information

Amount per serving	
Protein	40.5g
Fat	19.5g
Carbohydrates	43.9g
Fibre	7.3g
Energy	529kcal

Serves: 6
Prep time: 30 minutes,
plus up to 24 hours marinating time
Cooking time: 45 minutes

to brine the pork
200ml cold water
35g white miso paste
4 120g pork shoulder steaks
100g gochujang paste
50g blossom honey

for the broth
80ml dark soy sauce
20ml mirin
20ml rice wine
25g blossom honey
1 litre good quality chicken stock
3 cloves garlic, *peeled and minced*
30g ginger, *peeled and sliced*
30g dried porcini mushrooms
green tips from the spring onions

for the garnish
3 large eggs
3 pak choi, *sliced in half*
sunflower oil

to serve
4 carrots, *sliced into fine matchsticks*
180g red cabbage, *finely shredded*
300g cooked egg noodles
2 red chillies, *finely sliced*
1 bunch spring onions, *whites finely sliced (keep the green tops for the broth)*
4 radishes, *finely sliced*
nigella seeds
20g coriander leaves, *stalks removed*

Katsu is similar to German schnitzel and is one of the many Japanese dishes that has embraced Western influences, but adapted for local tastes. It was invented in the late 1800s by a Tokyo restaurant which wanted to serve a European-style meat cutlet with panko breadcrumbs. We've paired it with traditional sticky rice, broccoli, sugar snap peas and beansprouts to balance the dish.

KATSU CHICKEN WITH GARLIC AND CHILLI SUGAR SNAP PEAS AND STICKY RICE

For the chicken, slice the chicken lengthways to create two thin chicken steaks, making sure they're as equally-sized as possible. Place each half between two layers of cling film and using a meat hammer or rolling pin carefully flatten until an even 1cm thick. Put the flour, eggs and panko breadcrumbs in three separate bowls. Beat the eggs with 1 tablespoon of water and season the flour with salt, pepper and the curry powder. One piece at a time coat the chicken in the seasoned flour followed by the egg then the breadcrumbs, ensuring all the chicken is fully coated and there are no uncoated areas. Set aside on a lined baking tray.

For the katsu sauce, melt the butter in a saucepan over a medium heat, then add the flour and curry powder. Whisk to combine and cook for one minute until fragrant. Add the chicken stock a little at a time whisking continuously to ensure a smooth sauce. Whisk in the soy sauce and honey and set aside.

For the vegetables, place a large frying pan over a high heat and add the sesame oil. Once hot add the broccoli and stir fry for one minute, then add the sugar snaps and cook for 2 minutes until slightly blistered. Turn off the heat and stir through the beansprouts, garlic and chilli before seasoning to taste with salt and pepper.

For the sticky rice, rinse the rice in a sieve under cold running water until it runs clear. Place into a saucepan with the coconut milk and water. Place a lid on the saucepan and bring to a simmer over a medium-to-high heat. Once simmering, turn the heat as low as possible and cook for 10 minutes. Remove from the heat and leave covered for at least a further 20 minutes.

For the chicken, heat the oil in a large frying pan on a medium-to-high heat until hot – you can test the oil is ready by adding a few breadcrumbs to see if they sizzle straight away. Lower 2 piece of chicken slowly into the pan – be careful the hot oil doesn't splash you. Cook for 4-5 minutes, turning halfway through until golden brown. Repeat with the two remaining pieces of chicken.

To serve, divide the sticky rice between four bowls and top with the crispy chicken. Add the garlic and chilli sugar snaps to the bowls followed by a generous amount of the katsu curry sauce. Finish by garnishing with the coriander and gochugaru.

Nutritional information

Amount per serving	
Protein	49.8g
Fat	35.8g
Carbohydrates	88.7g
Fibre	8.6g
Energy	860kcal

Serves: 4
Prep time: 30 minutes
Cooking time: 35 minutes

for the chicken
2 large chicken breasts
50g plain flour
2 eggs
130g panko breadcrumbs
1 tbsp water
sea salt and cracked black pepper
1 tbsp mild curry powder

for the katsu sauce
50g unsalted butter
2 tbsps plain flour
2 tbsps mild curry powder
400ml chicken stock
1 tbsp soy sauce
1 tbsp honey

for the vegetables
1 tsp sesame oil
300g stem broccoli
300g sugar snap peas
100g beansprouts
2 garlic cloves, *peeled, finely sliced*
1 red chilli, *seeds removed, finely chopped*
sea salt and cracked black pepper

for the sticky rice
150g sushi rice
330ml coconut milk
50ml water

to serve
3 tbsps sunflower oil
10g coriander, *leaves only*
1 tsp gochugaru chilli flakes

A simple dish which was inspired by one of our favourite local restaurants, the Westwood in Beverley.

MISO AND SOY PORK CHOP, SESAME-GLAZED SUGAR SNAP PEAS AND MISO BOULANGÈRE POTATOES

For the pork chop marinade, in a bowl mix together the miso, shio koji, soy sauces and honey until smooth, then add the chilli and lime zest. With a sharp knife, remove the rind from the chops and add them to the marinade, making sure they're completely coated. Cover with cling film and place in the fridge for a minimum of 30 minutes, a maximum of 24 hours.

For the boulangère potatoes, preheat the oven to 180°C/350°F/gas mark 4. Add the oil and onions to a frying pan over a medium heat and cook for 3-4 minutes until softened but not turning brown. Either in four individual dishes or one larger dish, sprinkle some of the onions into the bottom followed by a layer of slightly overlapping potatoes. Season the potatoes and brush with a little of the butter. Repeat the layers until you are around 1cm from the top of the dish. In a pan heat the chicken stock and whisk in the miso paste until dissolved. Gently pour the stock over the potatoes, then top with a few drops of the remaining butter. Season and sprinkle over the fresh thyme leaves. Place in the oven for 60 minutes or until the potatoes have browned and are tender.

For the pork chops, when the potatoes are almost ready, remove the pork chops from the marinade, allowing any excess marinade to drip back into the bowl. Place them onto a clean plate ready for cooking. Keep the marinade for later to create a sticky soy and miso sauce. Add 2 tablespoons of vegetable oil to a frying pan over a medium-to-high heat. When the pan is hot, add the pork chops and cook for 30 seconds before flipping over – because of the honey and soy in the marinade the pork will colour quickly. Cook for another 30 seconds then flip over again. Add the butter to the pan and cook for another 30 seconds before flipping one more time. After another 30 seconds remove from the heat, transfer to a baking tray and pour the butter evenly over the chops. Place in the oven at 180°C/350°F/gas mark 4 for 8 minutes to fully cook through. Remove the pork from the oven, cover with tin foil and rest for 5 minutes before serving.

For the vegetables, add the oil to a frying pan over a high heat. Add the garlic, ginger, chilli and broccoli and fry for 1 minute. Add the sugar snaps and mix together, cook for another 2 minutes. Add the peas, soy sauce, sesame seeds, and coriander and cook for another minute. Season with sea salt and cracked black pepper.

For the sauce, place a saucepan on a medium-to-high heat. Add the marinating juices to the pan along with the honey and lime juice. Bring to the boil and then simmer for 2 minutes while stirring to thicken the sauce.

To serve, place a pork chop on each plate with a dish of boulangère potatoes. Spoon on some vegetables then finally drizzle with the sticky sauce.

Nutritional information

Amount per serving	
Protein	43.4g
Fat	42.0g
Carbohydrates	60.3g
Fibre	9.2g
Energy	772kcal

Serves: 4
Prep time: 20 minutes, *plus up to 24 hours marinating time*
Cooking time: 60 minutes

for the pork chops
10g white miso paste
10g shio koji
30ml light soy sauce
20ml dark soy sauce
30g clear honey
¼ red chilli, *seeds removed and finely chopped*
zest of 1 lime
4 thick cut pork chops, *rind removed*
2 tbsp vegetable oil
50g unsalted butter, *cut into 1cm cubes*

for the boulangère potatoes
1 tbsp extra virgin olive oil
2 white onions, *peeled and finely sliced*
360g floury potatoes, *such as Maris Piper or Desirée, peeled and finely sliced*
sea salt and cracked black pepper
40g unsalted butter, *melted*
300ml chicken stock
30g white miso paste
5g fresh thyme, *leaves only*

for the vegetables
10ml sesame oil
2 garlic cloves, *peeled and finely sliced*
20g fresh ginger, *peeled and finely chopped*
1 small red chilli, *seeds removed and finely chopped*
240g stem broccoli
320g sugar snap peas
150g frozen peas
20ml light soy sauce
1 tsp black sesame seeds
5g fresh coriander, *chopped*
sea salt and cracked black pepper

for the sauce
marinade juices, *from the chops*
60g clear honey
juice of 1 lime

Hot honey is one of the most on-trend sauces and flavour profiles of recent times. This dish incorporates hot honey with Asian flavours like miso, ginger, garlic and sriracha to make a really quick meal for any day of the week, which is perfect for sharing.

MISO, HOT HONEY PORK AND RICE NOODLE LETTUCE CUPS

Nutritional information

Amount per serving	
Protein	31.1g
Fat	18.7g
Carbohydrates	77.5g
Fibre	5.2g
Energy	772kcal

Serves: 4
Prep time: 20 minutes
Cooking time: 10 minutes

for the pork
20ml sunflower oil
4 garlic cloves, *peeled and finely chopped*
40g ginger, *peeled and finely chopped*
1 red chilli, *seeds removed and finely chopped*
500g pork mince
20g white miso
50g honey
40ml sriracha chilli sauce
10g coriander, *roughly chopped*

for the noodle salad
40ml light soy sauce
25ml rice wine vinegar
zest and juice of 1 lime
1 clove garlic, *peeled and finely grated*
60g honey
300g cooked vermicelli rice noodles
1 large carrot, *peeled and large grated*
20g coriander, *leaves only*
2 red chillies, *seeds removed and finely sliced*
3 spring onions, *roots removed and finely sliced*

for the dressing
80g honey
40ml sriracha chilli sauce
½ tsp sea salt
1 tsp black onion seeds

to serve
2 little gem lettuces, *root removed, washed and separated into leaves*

For the pork, place a frying pan on a medium-to-high heat, add the sunflower oil and the garlic, ginger and chilli. Fry gently, stirring, for one minute then add the pork mince. Continue stirring, breaking down the pork mince, for 5 minutes until the mince has separated and started to brown. Add the miso, honey and sriracha sauce and stir through the pork. Cook for another 4 minutes. Finally, add the chopped coriander and mix through.

For the noodle salad, in a bowl mix the soy sauce, rice wine vinegar, lime juice and zest, garlic and honey together and set aside. In another large mixing bowl add the noodles, carrot, coriander, chillies and spring onions. Toss the ingredients together to mix and then add the soy sauce mix.

For the dressing, in a small bowl mix the honey, sriracha, sea salt and black onion seeds and mix well. Set aside for later.

To serve, place four lettuce cups per person on each plate, fill with the vermicelli noodle salad and top with the miso pork mixture. Drizzle with the hot honey dressing.

Bo ssam is a Korean dish made from pork shoulder, boiled in broth and thinly sliced. Rooted in history, it was linked to the preparation of kimchi for winter. To ensure the commitment of the workers, the Yangban (elite scholars) would provide a pig for a feast, where the tender pork was served with newly made kimchi, still fresh and crisp. The pork and kimchi are wrapped in ssam vegetables (lettuce or leafy greens) giving the dish its name; 'bo ssam' means 'wrapped' in Korean.

PORK BO SSAM WITH STICKY RICE AND KIMCHI STIR FRY

Nutritional information

Amount per serving	
Protein	70.8g
Fat	52.0g
Carbohydrates	52.7g
Fibre	6.1g
Energy	979kcal

Serves: 6
Prep time: 20 minutes,
plus up to 24 hours marinating time
Cooking time: 4 hours 40 minutes

for the pork marinade
1.4kg pork shoulder
60g white sugar
60g sea salt
200ml chicken stock
4 tbsps brown sugar

for the sauce
2 tbsps sesame oil
10g ginger, *peeled and finely diced*
2 cloves garlic, *peeled and finely chopped*
2 tsps black onion seeds
4 tbsps ssamjang (soybean paste)
2 tbsps gochujang (fermented chilli paste)
1 tbsp honey
150ml water
30g spring onions, *thinly sliced*

for the rice
500g sushi rice
500ml water
1 tsp sea salt

for the stir fry
1 tbsp vegetable oil
480g stem broccoli
200g pak choi, *cut in half lengthways*
300g kimchi
300g beansprouts
100g spring onions, *finely chopped*
20g fresh coriander, *roughly chopped*

to serve
10g coriander, *leaves only*

To marinade the pork, mix the white sugar and salt together and cover the pork shoulder completely with it. Place the pork in a bowl, cover and leave in the fridge for at least two hours, preferably overnight.

Preheat the oven to 160°C/325°F/gas mark 3. Take the pork out of the fridge, place into a casserole dish with the chicken stock and cover the dish with foil to create a tight seal. Place in the oven for 4 hours. Take the pork out of the oven and carefully drain off any liquid in the bottom of the dish. Sprinkle over the brown sugar carefully, trying to coat the meat evenly. Turn the oven up to 180°C/350°F/gas mark 4 and put the pork back in for 25 minutes. Remove the pork from the oven once it has taken on a dark brown colour with lots of caramelisation and leave to rest for 15 minutes. Once rested, pull the pork with two forks into long shreds of meat.

For the sauce, place a frying pan with a little of the sesame oil over a medium heat. Add the ginger, garlic and black onion seeds and lightly fry until just starting to colour. Add the ssamjang, gochujang, remaining sesame oil, honey and water, mix well and bring to the boil. Remove the sauce from the heat and add the spring onions. Set aside.

For the rice, place the rice into a sieve and run under cold water until it runs clear. Place the rice into a saucepan and add the water and salt. Place over a medium-to-high heat and bring to the boil. Stir, then place the lid on the pan. Leave the heat on for 30 seconds to build up the temperature in the pan then switch off the heat, leaving the pan on the stove to absorb the water. Leave for 15 minutes with the lid on then remove the lid and fluff up the rice with a fork.

For the stir fry, place a frying pan or wok over a medium-to-high heat. Add the vegetable oil, the broccoli and pak choi. Fry for 4 minutes, tossing every minute. Add the kimchi, beansprouts, spring onions and coriander. Mix well whilst frying for another 90 seconds. Remove from the heat and serve immediately.

To serve, divide the sticky rice between six bowls and then add the stir fry. Place some pulled pork on top, pour over a little bit of ssam sauce and garnish with fresh coriander.

This recipe came about from one of my award-winning British BBQ competition dishes. I've taken Korean BBQ flavours and mixed them with American BBQ cooking methods to create a low and slow Korean pulled pork dish. Served with pit beans and corn on the cob that both have Korean-influenced flavours, this dish will take your barbecuing to the next level.

PULLED PORK WITH PIT BEANS AND CHARRED GOCHUJANG CORN ON THE COB

For the pork shoulder, place the pork joint onto a baking tray. Mix the gochujang and soy sauce together then brush the paste all over the pork. Mix together the sea salt, cracked black pepper, garlic powder, demerara sugar and Korean red pepper flakes to create a rub. Sprinkle the rub over the pork, turning over to ensure the base and the sides of the pork are seasoned. Leave to marinate whilst setting up the BBQ using the snake method, see page 173; you will need enough briquettes for half of the BBQ circumference (around a 5-hour cook). Light the BBQ. When it's reached a stable 125°C-130°C place the pork into the BBQ on the opposite side to the snake so the pork doesn't get any direct heat. Fill a heat-proof bowl or pan with water and place in the BBQ over the lit charcoals to create some steam. Place the lid back on and cook for 3 hours checking every 30 minutes; move the pork if needed away from the burning snake. At three hours the pork should be well coloured and ready to wrap. Place a double layer of foil on the worktop, put the honey, butter and water into the centre and place the pork on top. Wrap the pork tightly and place back in the BBQ for another 2-3 hours until the centre of the meat shows 93°C on a meat thermometer. Remove the meat from the BBQ and rest for an hour before serving.

For the pit beans, put a frying pan over a medium-to-high heat and add the bacon, onion and garlic and cook until starting to brown. Place the bacon mixture into an oven-proof dish along with all the other ingredients and stir together. Place the dish in the BBQ and cook for 60 minutes, stirring halfway through.

For the corn, cut the corn into 4 equal mini corn pinwheels. Place the corn into a bowl with all the other ingredients and mix together. Place the corn onto the BBQ and cook for 35-45 minutes until cooked and starting to brown.

For the BBQ sauce, in a bowl mix all the ingredients together well and set aside for later.

To serve, when the pork is ready, brush the meat fully with the BBQ sauce. Pull the meat apart with two forks and sprinkle with crispy onions and coriander then serve with the Korean pit beans and the corn.

Nutritional information

Amount per serving	
Protein	60.0g
Fat	26.0g
Carbohydrates	44.5g
Fibre	8.7g
Energy	690kcal

Serves: 8
Prep time: 20 minutes
Cooking time: 5-6 hours

for the pork shoulder

1.2kg pork shoulder joint (neck fillet)
1 tbsp gochujang
1 tbsp soy sauce
½ tbsp sea salt
1 tbsp cracked black pepper
1 tbsp garlic powder
1 tbsp demerara sugar
1 tbsp Korean red pepper flakes
2 tbsp honey
50g unsalted butter
80ml water

for the pit beans

10 rashers smoked dry-cured air-dried streaky bacon, *chopped*
1 onion, *peeled and finely diced*
4 garlic cloves, *peeled and finely sliced*
1 tin baked beans in tomato sauce
1 tin of black-eyed beans, *drained and washed*
80g gochujang
50ml red wine vinegar
30ml dark soy sauce
1 tsp fish sauce
80g clear honey
50g unsalted butter
1 tsp black onion seeds
sea salt and cracked black pepper

for the corn

2 corn cobs
1 tbsp extra virgin olive oil
1 tbsp gochujang
1 tsp Korean red pepper flakes
1 tbsp honey
sea salt and cracked black pepper

for the BBQ sauce

100g BBQ sauce
1 tbsp gochujang
1 tbsp dark soy sauce
1 tsp fish sauce
1 tbsp honey
1 tsp black onion seeds
1 lime, *juice and zest*
5g coriander, *finely chopped*

for the garnish

80g crispy onions
10g fresh coriander leaves

Chicken wings are great carriers for high impact flavours and this recipe is no exception. It was inspired by street food and would usually be served with loaded fries. To make the dish healthier and more balanced, we've used new potato wedges which are quick to cook but still just as tasty as classic fries. The Chinese-flavoured BBQ sauce drizzled over the wings is just finger-licking good!

SALT AND CHILLI CHICKEN WINGS WITH LOADED NEW POTATO WEDGES

Nutritional information

Amount per serving	
Protein	49.2g
Fat	31.9g
Carbohydrates	60.5g
Fibre	5.6g
Energy	714kcal

Serves: 4
Prep time: 30 minutes,
plus up to 24 hours marinating time
Cooking time: 40 minutes

for the chicken
1kg chicken wings
10g salt

for the salt and chilli seasoning
10g salt
10g caster sugar
5g chilli flakes
40g cornflour
5g cracked white pepper
5g ground black pepper

for the pickled red onions
50g caster sugar
100ml white wine vinegar
100ml water
1 red onion, *peeled and finely sliced*
1 red chilli, *thinly sliced*

for the BBQ sauce
50ml oyster sauce
25ml soy sauce
50ml hoisin sauce
1 tbsp caster sugar
½ tsp sesame oil
zest of 1 orange
zest and juice of 1 lime

for the wings and wedges
480g new potatoes, *cut into wedges*
2 tbsps vegetable oil
salt and chilli seasoning

to serve
2 spring onions, *finely chopped*
black onion seeds
sesame seeds

To prepare the chicken, place the chicken wings in a large bowl and add the salt. Mix until well coated and leave for 1 hour before rinsing off the salt and drying thoroughly. Place on a wire rack with a tray underneath ensuring they are spaced apart and leave uncovered in the fridge overnight to dry the skin out.

For the salt and chilli seasoning, place the salt, sugar, chilli flakes, cornflour and white and black pepper in a small bowl. Mix well until combined. You'll be using half of this for the chicken, the other half for the potato wedges.

For the pickled red onions, add the sugar, vinegar and water to a saucepan and bring to a boil. Add the red onion and chilli to the pan. Remove from the heat and leave for at least two hours.

For the BBQ sauce, combine the oyster, soy and hoisin sauces with the sugar in a small saucepan and bring to a simmer. Remove from the heat and add the sesame oil, orange zest, lime zest and juice then mix well. Set aside to cool until ready to serve.

To cook the wings and wedges, preheat the oven to 220°C/425°F/gas mark 7. Add the wings and potatoes to two separate large bowls, add 1 tablespoon of vegetable oil to each bowl and toss to thoroughly coat. Add half the salt and chilli seasoning to each bowl and toss again. Transfer the wings and wedges to separate lined baking trays and bake for 35-40 minutes until golden and crispy.

To serve, transfer the wings and wedges to a large serving board, drizzle over the BBQ sauce and drain and scatter over the pickled red onions, spring onions, black onion seeds and sesame seeds.

This stir fry recipe is a taste explosion that ticks all of the flavour boxes! It's sweet, sour, spicy and salty and uses traditional Szechuan pepper flakes and thinly sliced pork fillet that is really tender, healthy and super quick to cook. The Szechuan pepper flakes give this dish its authentic flavour of citrus, pepper and spice.

SZECHUAN PORK STIR FRY

For the Szechuan sauce, combine all of the ingredients and whisk together until thoroughly combined. Set aside.

For the stir fry, bring a pan of water to the boil, add the noodles, cook for 6-8 minutes, then drain and set aside.

Place a wok or large sauté pan over a medium-to-high heat and add a good drizzle of extra virgin olive oil. Place the pork strips in the pan and caramelise until the meat has a nice, browned colour. Add the vegetables and cook for two minutes over a high heat. Add the drained noodles and toss together everything until combined. Add the Szechuan sauce and mix thoroughly. Cook for a further 2 minutes to thicken the sauce.

To serve, portion the stir fry into 4 bowls and garnish with coriander, sesame seeds, chillies and spring onions. Season with sea salt and cracked black pepper.

Nutritional information

Amount per serving	
Protein	39.5g
Fat	12.2g
Carbohydrates	44.2g
Fibre	6.6g
Energy	435kcal

Serves: 6
Prep time: 20 minutes
Cooking time: 10-15 minutes

for the Szechuan sauce

½ tsp Szechuan pepper flakes, or red pepper flakes
250ml low sodium soy sauce
2 tbsps maple syrup
1 tbsp cornflour
2 tbsps tomato paste
1 tsp garlic purée
½ tsp chilli paste
1 tbsp rice vinegar
½ tsp Chinese five spice
1 tsp ginger paste

for the stir fry

250g dried medium egg noodles
1 tbsp extra virgin olive oil
800g pork tenderloin, *cut into thin strips*
150g sugar snap peas
1 red bell pepper, *finely sliced*
1 yellow bell pepper, *finely sliced*
1 bunch spring onions, *roughly chopped*
1 red chilli, *seeds removed and finely sliced*
1 red onion, *peeled and finely sliced*
200g pak choi, *cut into quarters*
300g beansprouts
300g stem broccoli

to serve

20g coriander, *roughly chopped*
1 tsp black sesame seeds
2 red chillies, *finely sliced, seeds included*
2 spring onions, finely sliced
sea salt and cracked black pepper

This recipe cooks the chicken skewers on the BBQ, so you get great flavour from the coals, while continuously brushing the chicken with teriyaki sauce builds flavour and creates a thick glossy glaze on the outside. The citrussy yuzu dressing on the salad perfectly complements the sweet teriyaki sauce.

TERIYAKI CHICKEN WITH EDAMAME BEAN AND YUZU NOODLE SALAD

For the marinade, mix the soy, sugar, garlic and ginger in a large bowl until the sugar has dissolved. Add the chicken and coat thoroughly in the marinade. Cover and refrigerate for a minimum of 6 hours, ideally overnight.

For the sauce, place all the ingredients in a small saucepan and bring to a simmer. Gently simmer for 5 minutes or until reduced by half, then remove from the heat and allow to cool.

For the yuzu dressing, combine all the ingredients in a small mixing bowl and whisk together until emulsified.

For the noodle salad, combine all the ingredients in a large bowl and pour over the yuzu dressing and mix well.

For the chicken, place your wooden skewers into a bowl of water an hour before skewering; this will stop them from burning when cooking. Set up your BBQ for direct cooking, see page 174. Remove the chicken from the marinade and skewer on to the soaked wooden skewers. Place onto the BBQ and grill for 2-3 minutes per side. Brush with the sauce and turn again for a further minute. Repeat 5 times until each piece of chicken is well caramelised and glazed with the sauce.

To serve, divide the noodle salad between four plates and top with the glazed chicken skewers.

Nutritional information

Amount per serving	
Protein	53.5g
Fat	17.9g
Carbohydrates	66.8g
Fibre	8.1g
Energy	625kcal

Serves: 4
Prep time: 30 minutes,
plus up to 24 hours marinating time
Cooking time: 15 minutes

for the marinade
60ml tamari soy sauce
30g brown sugar
2 garlic cloves, *peeled and grated*
10g ginger, *peeled and grated*
600g chicken mini fillets

for the sauce
5g ginger, *peeled and grated*
1 spring onion, *finely sliced*
1 garlic clove, *peeled and grated*
60ml tamari soy sauce
60ml mirin
30g brown sugar

for the yuzu dressing
½ tsp togorashi
2 tsps mirin
2 tsps honey
½ tsp sesame oil
20ml yuzu juice

for the noodle salad
300g cooked rice noodles
175g cooked edamame beans
15g beansprouts
150g carrot, *peeled and finely sliced*
2 spring onions, *finely sliced*
10g coriander, *roughly chopped*
150g peanuts
1 small red chilli, *thinly sliced*

Beer can-smoked chicken with bacon-wrapped asparagus and broccoli and hot new potato salad – *USA*

Jerk BBQ chicken with rice and peas – *Jamaican*

Kalua pork shoulder with cabbage, charred pineapple and luau rice – *Hawaiian*

BBQ oak-smoked low 'n' slow Boston butt pulled pork rolls – *USA*

Pork pibil with guacamole, tomato salsa and pickled red onions – *Mexican*

THE AMERICAS

The discovery of fire is credited b
step in the evolution of mankinc
would have been the first form c
digest our food. The practice has bee
Pork and chicken are perfect fc
on flavour, absorbing smokines
The Americans are evangelical abou
USA, Mexico and Hawaii are centra

ome anthropologists as a crucial
Heating food over fire and coals
ooking, helping us to sanitise and
ound across all cultures over centuries.
arbecuing due to the way they take
rom the coals and open flame.
ne BBQ and these recipes from the
o their unique food culture and history

Cooking with fire – Simon Woods

I'm excited to share my passion and expertise in all things BBQ. Whether you're a seasoned grill master or just starting out, this guide will walk you through essential BBQ techniques, the best fuels to use for different types of cooking, and even debunk some common BBQ myths along the way. Having competed at the World BBQ Championships in Memphis USA and the UK BBQ Championships in 2023 and 2024, where my team very proudly claimed the title of Grand Champions, I've learnt a thing or two about what makes a great BBQ experience. Now, I'm thrilled to pass on that knowledge to help elevate your own backyard barbecuing!

In the UK, BBQ fever strikes hard during those rare sunny days, sending us all rushing to the supermarkets to grab anything we can throw on the grill. However, the most common complaint I hear from BBQ enthusiasts is about over-cooking or burning food. Fortunately, this is an easy problem to solve with just a few simple adjustments to your BBQ technique. One of the biggest mistakes people make is loading up their BBQ with too much charcoal and setting it ablaze, creating a heat so intense it could rival the sun. This often leads to food that's charred on the outside but undercooked in the middle, a BBQ disaster I'm going to help you avoid.

So, let's start with the basics, beginning with the humble yet iconic kettle BBQ. This design has been improved over the years and remains a versatile, cost-effective choice for a wide range of cooking styles. Throughout this book, I'll use a kettle BBQ as our reference point for setup and cooking tips, guiding you to BBQ success with every cook.

Types of fuel

Charcoal

Charcoal briquettes – Typically made from compressed sawdust, wood chips, coal dust, or other organic materials bound together with additives like starch. They're uniform in size and shape, which allows for more consistent heat distribution during cooking. They often burn for a longer period and at a more stable temperature compared to lumpwood charcoal and are suitable for cooking foods that require longer cooking times or more even heat, such as slow-cooked meats, smoking, or indirect grilling.

Lumpwood charcoal – Made from natural hardwood such as oak, hickory, maple, or mesquite that is burned in the absence of oxygen to create carbonised wood. It tends to produce a higher heat output and burns hotter than briquettes, making it ideal for searing and grilling foods quickly. It often imparts a more intense and authentic smoky flavour to grilled foods compared to briquettes and may vary in size and shape, which can lead to uneven heat distribution and shorter burn times compared to briquettes.

Wood

A great way to add flavour to your food when cooking with a kettle BBQ is to add in the odd chunk of wood or scatter on some wood chips to the burning embers of charcoal.

Oak – Offers a medium to strong flavour that is relatively neutral compared to other woods. It's versatile and works well with a wide range of meats, including beef, pork and poultry. It's often used as a base wood in smoking blends or combined with other woods to add depth of flavour.

Applewood – Offers a mild and sweet flavour with a subtle fruitiness. It's a versatile wood that pairs well with a variety of meats, including pork, poultry and fish. It is especially popular for smoking chicken and pork ribs.

Cherry – Provides a sweet and fruity flavour with a hint of tartness. It's excellent for smoking pork, poultry and beef, adding a beautiful mahogany colour to the meat. It can complement both sweet and savoury dishes.

Ash – Offers a mild and slightly sweet flavour with subtle hints of nuttiness. It's a relatively neutral wood that can complement a variety of meats without overpowering their natural flavours. It burns cleanly and evenly, making it a good choice for smoking delicate foods like fish or vegetables and can add a subtle smokiness to dishes.

Birch – Provides a light and sweet flavour with subtle hints of wintergreen or mint. It's ideal for smoking poultry, pork and seafood, adding a delicate smokiness without overwhelming the natural flavours. It burns quickly and produces a moderate amount of smoke, making it suitable for shorter cooking times or lighter smoking applications.

Types of cooking

Indirect cooking setup

(page 175, top left image)

Fuel – Briquettes for longer cooks, lumpwood for quick cooks, wood chunks or chips optional.

Kettle BBQ method – Fill up a starter chimney with good quality briquettes or lumpwood charcoal. Place a natural firelighter and some small bits of kindling on the lower grill grate in your BBQ, light the firelighter then place your starter chimney on top of the fire. Ensure the vents are fully open on the base of the BBQ. Place another pile of charcoal on the lower grill grate ready to empty your chimney on top. After 15-20 minutes your chimney starter should be very hot and charcoal glowing red. Very carefully pour out your chimney over the unlit pile of charcoal. If any fall off the pile, using some tongs pile up the glowing charcoal, keeping a nice tidy pile to one side of the BBQ. Place your cooking grill grate on the BBQ and close the lid and allow the charcoal and temperature to settle for 10 minutes. To reduce the temperature in the BBQ you will need to close up the vent on the bottom of the BBQ; this will reduce the air flow through the BBQ, in time, reducing the temperature in the BBQ. If you want to add some smoke flavour, drop on a couple of wood chunks of your choice or a handful of wood chips onto the glowing coals just before you start your cook.

Low and slow, snake method setup

(page 175, top right image)

Fuel – Briquettes.

Kettle BBQ method – To set up the snake method on a kettle BBQ, start by arranging unlit charcoal briquettes in a semi-circle around the edge of the grill, forming a "snake" shape. The snake should be two briquettes wide and two high. Depending on what you are cooking the snake should run about halfway or three-quarters around the perimeter of the grill. This setup allows for a slow, steady burn, perfect for low and slow cooking. Next, add wood chunks on top of the briquettes along the snake. Cherry wood chunks are my go-to wood on the snake as they give really good colour and a subtle not overly smoky flavour to the meat. The wood chunks will gradually ignite as the charcoal burns along the snake. Place a few chunks at intervals along the length of the snake for consistent smoke throughout the cooking process. Place 8 to 10 good quality charcoal briquettes in your starter chimney. Place a natural firelighter and some small bits of kindling on the lower grill grate in your BBQ, light the firelighter then place your starter chimney on top of the fire. Ensure the vents are fully open on the base of the BBQ. Once these briquettes are hot and covered in ash, carefully place them at the beginning of the snake using metal tongs.

This will start the burn and the lit coals will gradually ignite the unlit briquettes and wood chunks, creating a slow, controlled burn. Finally, position a drip pan/tray filled with water in the centre of the grill, underneath where your food will be placed. This helps regulate the temperature, keeps a moist environment and catches any drips. Place the cooking grate back on the grill and position your food above the drip pan, away from the direct heat. Close the lid (you can adjust the vents on the bottom of the BBQ to control the airflow) and monitor the temperature to maintain a low, steady heat for slow cooking.

Direct cooking setup

(opposite page, bottom right image)

Fuel – Lumpwood for hot and fast cooks.

Kettle BBQ method – Fill up a starter chimney with good quality lumpwood charcoal. Place a natural firelighter and some small bits of kindling on the lower grill grate in your BBQ, light the firelighter then place your starter chimney on top of the fire. Ensure the vents are fully open on the base of the BBQ. Place another pile of lumpwood charcoal on the lower grate ready to empty your starter chimney onto. When the coals are glowing red very carefully empty the starter chimney over the pile of unlit coals and then spread out evenly on the base of the grill grate. Leave the BBQ lid off and allow the other coals to catch. When most of the coals have turned white you are ready to cook, this should take another 10-15 minutes.

Wrap up

Wrapping up this little guide to the world of BBQ, I hope you're feeling fired up and ready to conquer your BBQ like never before. Whether you're grilling sausages to perfection on a rare sunny day in the UK or slow-cooking juicy pulled pork, remember that great BBQ isn't just about the food, it's about the fun, the flavours and maybe even a little bit of smoke in your eyes.

With the tips and techniques from this guide and the BBQ recipes in the book now in your toolkit, you're well on your way to becoming the neighbourhood BBQ guru. So go ahead, embrace the heat, experiment with those wood chunks and let your BBQ skills shine. Just try not to set anything on fire – except the charcoal, of course. Happy grilling!

BBQ culture is a deeply ingrained American tradition, and one of its stand-out dishes is beer can smoked chicken. Popularised by BBQ guru Steve Raichlen in the mid-1990s after he encountered it at the World BBQ Championships in Memphis, this dish has since become a staple in the BBQ scene. While its roots can be traced to Louisiana, variations of the recipe also emerged around the same time in Mississippi, Texas and Kansas, each adding its own regional twist. The beer keeps the chicken moist whilst grilling and it has become a popular method across America.

BEER CAN SMOKED CHICKEN WITH BACON-WRAPPED ASPARAGUS AND BROCCOLI AND HOT NEW POTATO SALAD

Nutritional information

Amount per serving	
Protein	75.7g
Fat	50.0g
Carbohydrates	48.1g
Fibre	6.1g
Energy	970kcal

Serves: 6
Prep time: 20 minutes
Cooking time: 2 hours 5 minutes

for the beer can chicken
1.4kg whole chicken
440ml can of your favourite beer (I use Brewdog's Mr President)
1 tbsp extra virgin olive oil
sea salt and cracked black pepper

for the BBQ sauce
440ml can of your favourite beer
125g tomato ketchup
40g American mustard
40g wholegrain mustard
50ml cider vinegar
75ml soy sauce
30ml Worcestershire sauce
65g dark brown muscovado sugar
1 tsp smoked paprika
1 tsp cracked black pepper
1 tsp garlic powder
1 tsp onion powder

for the hot potato salad
640g new potatoes
2 tbsps extra virgin olive oil
12 rashers smoked dry cured air-dried streaky bacon, *chopped*
1 onion, *peeled and diced into 1cm pieces*
2 tbsps wholegrain mustard
15g fresh dill
juice and zest of 1 lemon
sea salt and cracked black pepper

for the asparagus and broccoli
12 rashers of smoked dry cured air-dried streaky bacon
12 asparagus stems, *woody stalk removed*
360g stem broccoli
1 tbsp extra virgin olive oil
cracked black pepper

For the beer can chicken, prepare your BBQ for cooking using the indirect heat method, see page 173, looking for a 140°C temperature and add a bowl of water to the BBQ for steam. Place the chicken on a large baking tray and pour 2 tablespoons of the beer and the olive oil over it, rubbing them in. Season well all over with salt and pepper. Put the chicken onto the open can of beer, legs down, so that it looks as if it's sitting upright with the can in its cavity. Place the chicken in the BBQ and smoke for 2 hours. Using a meat thermometer, check the temperature of the chicken after two hours; you're looking for a minimum of 75°C in the thickest parts of the legs near the bones. When up to temperature, brush the chicken with the BBQ sauce and close the lid again for 5 minutes. Remove the bird from the BBQ and allow to rest for 15 minutes before serving.

For the BBQ sauce, in a saucepan reduce the beer by a third over a medium heat. Add the remaining ingredients and mix together well. Continue stirring until the sauce comes to the boil. Remove from the heat and set aside for later.

For the hot potato salad, place the potatoes in a saucepan, cover with cold water and season with salt. Place on a medium heat and bring to the boil. Reduce the heat and simmer for 10-15 minutes until the potatoes are cooked and tender. Drain and set aside. Place a frying pan on a medium heat and add the oil, bacon and onion. Fry until starting to turn brown then add the wholegrain mustard, dill, lemon juice and zest and season with salt and cracked black pepper. Mix together, then add the potatoes. Mix the potatoes through the mustard mix gently until fully coated.

For the asparagus and broccoli, on a chopping board place two rashers of streaky bacon side by side. Place two asparagus stems and two broccoli stems on one end of the bacon then roll the bacon tightly around the outside of the vegetables. To cook, brush the parcels with oil and season with cracked black pepper and place on the BBQ directly over the coals, turning every 2 minutes until the bacon is crisp.

To serve, carve the chicken breasts, remove the legs and wings and serve with the potatoes and asparagus and broccoli wraps, then finish with the BBQ sauce.

Jerk is a key part of Jamaican cultural identity and dates back to the 17th century. It reflects the history of the Maroons' resistance against slavery. The Maroons were the Jamaican descendants of African tribes like the Ashanti and Fante, who fled to the mountains in search of freedom and used jerk seasoning to preserve meat while hiding from colonial forces. The vibrant mix of locally sourced spices, including allspice, Scotch Bonnet peppers, thyme and garlic creates the distinctive flavour of jerk. The seasoned and preserved meat was then slow-cooked over a low fire to develop its smoky, spicy taste.

JERK BBQ CHICKEN WITH RICE AND PEAS

For the jerk chicken, make a marinade by placing all the ingredients except the chicken into a blender and blend until smooth. Cut some deep lines into the top of the chicken legs to allow the marinade to get inside the meat. Rub the marinade all over the chicken legs making sure to get into the cuts, place in a bowl, cover with cling film and leave for at least 2 hours to marinate (preferably overnight). Set up the BBQ for indirect cooking, see page 173, at a temperature of 180°C-200°C. Place the chicken onto a lined baking tray and onto the BBQ away from the coals and cook for 35 minutes, then place the chicken in the grill directly over the coals for another 10 minutes to char, turning every 2 minutes. Check with a meat thermometer that you have reached 85°C in the thickest part of the leg. Place back on the tray, cover with foil and rest for 5 minutes before serving.

For the rice and peas, wash the rice thoroughly and allow to fully drain. Place in a pan over a low heat to toast slightly for 6 minutes, stirring constantly. Add the kidney beans, coconut milk, thyme, garlic, allspice, spring onions and Scotch Bonnet and let simmer for 30 minutes, with the lid slightly ajar. Remove from the heat and let it steam with the lid on for 10 minutes. Fluff up the rice with a fork.

To serve, divide the rice and peas between four plates and place a chicken leg on top. Sprinkle with chopped coriander and finely sliced Scotch Bonnet chilli, season with sea salt and cracked black pepper and add half a lime to squeeze over the chicken.

Nutritional information

Amount per serving	
Protein	51.6g
Fat	37.2g
Carbohydrates	63.7g
Fibre	8.5g
Energy	782kcal

Serves: 4
Prep time: 20 minutes,
plus up to 24 hours marinating time
Cooking time: 50 minutes

for the jerk chicken
4 skin-on chicken legs
4 Scotch Bonnet peppers, *seeds removed*
1 white onion, *peeled and roughly chopped*
5 garlic cloves, *peeled*
4 spring onions, *root removed and roughly chopped*
60 ml soy sauce
50 ml red wine vinegar
juice of 1 orange
juice of 1 lime
1 tbsp fresh ginger, *peeled*
2 tbsps brown sugar
2 tbsps honey
1 tsp fresh thyme leaves
1 tsp ground allspice
1 tsp ground nutmeg
1 tsp ground cinnamon

for the rice and peas
200g long grain rice
400g red kidney beans, *drained*
400ml full fat coconut milk
4 sprigs fresh thyme
2 garlic cloves, *peeled and finely chopped*
1 tsp ground allspice
4 spring onions, *finely chopped*
½ Scotch Bonnet pepper, *seeds removed and finely chopped*

for the garnish
15g coriander, *roughly chopped*
1 red Scotch Bonnet pepper, *finely sliced*
sea salt and cracked black pepper
2 limes, *cut in half*

In ancient Hawaii men and women ate meals separately following the Kapu (taboo) system which governed their way of life; this ended in 1819 when King Kamehameha held a feast where he ate with women, thus ending the Kapu. Word spread across the Islands of the first lu'au and the larger Aha'aina feasts began where men and women ate together. In Hawaii, this pork dish was wrapped in banana leaves then cooked in an underground oven or imu. The rich and smoky kalua pork is coated in Hawaiian sea salt, balancing the sweetness of the pork fat. The lu'au rice is a colourful and tasty accompaniment to the pulled kalua pork, which is drizzled with cooking juices from the bottom of the dish.

KALUA PORK SHOULDER WITH CABBAGE, CHARRED PINEAPPLE AND LUAU RICE

Nutritional information

Amount per serving	
Protein	66.8g
Fat	25.3g
Carbohydrates	57.6g
Fibre	6.1g
Energy	714kcal

Serves: 6
Prep time: 20 minutes
Cooking time: 6 hours

for the kalua pork
1.5kg boneless rind-off pork shoulder
1 tbsp vegetable oil
2 tbsps Hawaiian volcanic salt (alternatively smoked sea salt)
3-4 banana leaves
500ml chicken stock

for the cabbage
1 large Savoy cabbage
1 tsp vegetable oil
½ tsp sesame oil
1 tsp soy sauce

for the pickled chillies
80g caster sugar
100ml white wine vinegar
100ml water
3 red chillies

for the rice
400g sweet potato, *peeled and diced*
1 tbsp extra virgin olive oil
sea salt and cracked black pepper
50g butter
400ml chicken stock
1 tsp chilli flakes
200g pineapple, *chopped*
½ tsp salt
½ tsp white granulated sugar
200g basmati rice
10g coriander, *chopped*
zest and juice of 1 lime

to serve
1 small pineapple
10g coriander
1 tbsp sesame seeds

For the kalua pork, preheat the oven to 160°C/325°F/gas mark 3, or set up the BBQ for indirect cooking, see page 173, and regulate the temperature for 160°C. Place a large casserole dish over a high heat on the stove or directly over the coals. When hot add the vegetable oil and sear the pork shoulder on all sides until well coloured. Remove the dish from the heat and take out the pork. Generously season with the Hawaiian salt and wrap in the banana leaves before returning it to the dish along with the stock. If cooking in the oven cover with a lid and place into the pre-heated oven for 5 hours. If cooking on the BBQ leave the lid off whilst cooking to help develop the smoky flavour and place the dish away from the hot coals and cook for 5 hours until tender. Once cooked remove from the oven or BBQ and rest for another hour.

For the cabbage, quarter and remove the core from the cabbage before slicing about 1cm thick. Place a large frying pan over a high heat and once hot add 1 teaspoon of vegetable oil and the sliced cabbage. Cook for 5 to 6 minutes until lightly charred and wilted, then add the sesame oil and soy sauce and stir through before removing from the heat.

For the pickled chillies, add the sugar, vinegar and water to a saucepan and bring to a boil. Thinly slice the chillies and add the pan. Remove from the heat and leave for at least two hours.

For the rice, preheat the oven to 180°C/350°F/gas mark 4. Place the sweet potatoes on a baking tray and add the olive oil, mixing to coat, then season with salt and pepper. Put in the oven for 20 minutes until starting to brown. Add the butter, chicken stock, chilli flakes, pineapple, salt and sugar to a large saucepan with a lid. Place the saucepan over a medium heat, bring to a simmer, add the rice and stir. Reduce the heat to low and replace the lid. Cook for 15 minutes then remove from the heat leaving the lid on and steam for a further 10 minutes. Finish by lightly fluffing with a fork, adding the chopped coriander and the lime zest and juice and topping with the roasted sweet potatoes.

To serve, remove the skin from the pineapple and slice into eight large pieces lengthways, discarding the core. Place a griddle pan on a high heat and char the pineapple for 2 to 3 minutes on each side. Remove the pork from the banana leaves and pull apart using two forks. Add a good helping of the rice to a bowl along with the cabbage and charred pineapple. Finish by topping with the kalua pork, drizzling over any cooking juices, then garnish the dish with the coriander, pickled chillies and a sprinkle of sesame seeds.

If you really want to impress at your next BBQ, this is the recipe for you. It uses a traditional US cut of pork called the Boston butt, a large piece of the pork shoulder that still has the shoulder blade bone inside. The meat is rubbed with a classic BBQ marinade of smoked paprika, salt, pepper and garlic powder which will give the meat a great colour and a dark, crisp exterior. I've used chunks of oak wood on the BBQ to create a deep red smoke ring on the pork – the sign of any great low and slow BBQ meat.

BBQ OAK-SMOKED LOW 'N' SLOW BOSTON BUTT PULLED PORK ROLLS

Nutritional information

Amount per serving	
Protein	66.7g
Fat	54.1g
Carbohydrates	60.0g
Fibre	6.0g
Energy	984kcal

Serves: 18-20
Prep time: 10 minutes
Cooking time: 12-13 hours

for the Boston butt
1 5-6kg Boston butt (pork shoulder), rindless
2 tbsps smoked paprika
1 tbsp sea salt
2 tbsps cracked black pepper
2 tbsps garlic powder
250g unsalted butter
100g clear honey
100ml apple juice

for the slaw
1 small red cabbage, *finely sliced*
1 onion, *peeled and finely sliced*
1 large carrot, *peeled and grated*
4 tbsps crème fraîche
10g parsley leaves, *roughly chopped*
zest of 1 lemon
sea salt and cracked black pepper

for the garnish
20 crusty rolls
250g unsalted butter
280g mixed leaf salad

For the Boston butt, place the pork onto a baking tray. Mix together the smoked paprika, sea salt, cracked black pepper and garlic powder. Sprinkle the marinade over the pork so all of it is seasoned. Leave to marinate whilst setting up the BBQ using the snake method, see page 173. You will need enough briquettes for two-thirds of the BBQ – around a 12-hour cook. Add some oak wood chunks around the first half of the charcoal snake. When you have a stable 125°C -130°C place the pork into the BBQ on the opposite side to the snake so the pork doesn't get any direct heat. Fill a heatproof bowl or pan with water and place in the BBQ over the lit charcoals to create some steam. Place the lid back on. Keep checking the BBQ and the colour of your pork, with a stable temperature you should be cooking the butt for 5 hours. Remove the pork and wrap, fat side up, in a triple layer of foil or a double layer of butcher's paper, adding the butter, honey and apple juice. Make sure the wrap is tight but be careful not to puncture the foil or paper: you don't want to lose any of the juices. Place the butt back onto the BBQ and cook for another 6-7 hours. After 3 hours check the pork every hour with a meat thermometer. When the meat reaches 93°C in the centre remove it from the BBQ and allow to rest for a minimum of one hour.

For the slaw, mix all the ingredients together and season with sea salt and cracked black pepper.

To serve, using two forks pull all the meat off the bones (the bones will easily pull out of the meat and can be discarded). Drizzle with some of the cooking juices. Butter the rolls and add some salad, slaw and the pulled pork.

Mexican pork pibil is a traditional Mexican street food from the Yucatan Peninsula, a Mayan slow-roasted pork dish normally served with tortillas for a sharing-style feast. The original 'conchita pibil' (conchita means baby pig) involved marinading the meat in strong citrus juice and annatto seeds which gives it its famous burnt orange colour. Traditionally buried in a pit with fire at the bottom to roast, it's served with corn tortillas, pickled red onions, refried black beans and Habanero chillies.

PORK PIBIL WITH GUACAMOLE, TOMATO SALSA AND PICKLED RED ONIONS

Nutritional information

Amount per serving	
Protein	59.0g
Fat	42.2g
Carbohydrates	66.2g
Fibre	10.7g
Energy	862kcal

Serves: 6
Prep time: 15 minutes,
plus up to 24 hours marinating time
Cooking time: 5-6 hours

for the pibil
1 tbsp achiote or chipotle paste
5 garlic cloves, *peeled and finely chopped*
1 tbsp dried oregano
1 tsp dried chilli flakes
2 tsps smoked paprika
sea salt and cracked black pepper
juice of 3 limes
juice of 2 oranges
1kg pork shoulder joint, *boneless and rindless*

for the guacamole
2 ripe avocados, *peeled, stone removed and mashed*
juice of 1 lime
1 small red onion, *peeled and finely chopped*
10g coriander, *finely chopped*

for the salsa
4 large tomatoes, *seeds removed, diced*
1 red onion, *peeled and diced*
20g coriander leaves, *roughly chopped*
1 red jalapeño, *seeds removed and finely chopped*
200g tinned black beans, *drained and rinsed*
50g sweetcorn kernels
juice of 1 lime
1 tsp cumin
1 tsp smoked paprika
sea salt and cracked black pepper

for the pickled onions
6 tbsps red wine vinegar
2 large red onions, *peeled and finely sliced*

to serve
12 tortilla wraps

For the pibil, place the achiote or chipotle paste into a bowl and add the dry ingredients. Add the lime and orange juice and mix well. Wearing gloves, add the meat to the marinade and mix thoroughly: you can do this in advance and leave overnight for an enhanced flavour.

Preheat the oven to 140°C/275°F/gas mark 1. Place the marinated meat and all the juices into an ovenproof dish, cover tightly with foil and place in the oven for 5-6 hours. Bake until the meat is falling apart and easy to shred.

Carefully transfer the meat to a dish, retaining the cooking juices. Pull the meat apart with two forks, adding some of the cooking juices to stop it drying out.

For the guacamole, place the mashed avocados into a bowl and squeeze over the lime juice to stop it going black. Mix in the red onion and coriander. Serve immediately or put in the fridge covered with cling film for up to 24 hours.

For the salsa, place the diced tomatoes in a bowl and add the remaining ingredients. Stir to combine and set aside for at least an hour for the flavours to develop. This could be made a day before and refrigerated.

For the pickled onions, heat the vinegar in a saucepan over a medium heat. Just before it comes to the boil, remove from the heat and stir through the onions. Cover the pan with cling film and leave for 15 minutes to pickle.

To serve, place the tortilla wraps into tin foil and put in the oven to warm. Place the pulled pork pibil alongside the salsa and pickled red onions on a board. To build the wraps, spread some guacamole onto each wrap, top with pork, salsa and red onions then wrap up tightly.

Chicken

Lamb

Pork

Jim Brisby

Jim was born in Yorkshire with family ties to farming and the pig industry and has worked in the food industry for his entire career since joining Cranswick in 1995.

His first role was to bring gourmet sausages to the mass market, alongside Martin Heap of Simply Sausages, helping establish the premium sausage sector, which now accounts for half of all UK sausage sales. This set the blueprint for working with local artisan producers to bring their products to supermarkets' premium brands, with the Jack Scaife hand-cured and air-dried bacon following some years later, as well as the Woodall's British Charcuterie products and handmade pastry products from Yorkshire Baker.

Jim's extensive knowledge of the meat industry, coupled with his passion for delivering quality and innovative food to consumers both at home and in the market, has been instrumental in driving Cranswick's growth and shaping its strategic direction.

His commitment to sustainability inspired the creation of the group's sustainability strategy, Second Nature, which has positioned Cranswick as a leader in understanding and addressing the environmental impacts – and benefits – of food and livestock production.

In addition to his role at Cranswick, Jim serves on the AHDB Pig Sector Council, a levy body that supports and promotes the UK pig industry domestically and internationally.

Jim was inspired to write Omnivore by his belief and passion that meat and fresh produce should form the foundations of our diet and that everyone deserves better food.

Simon Woods

Simon started his career at The Savoy Hotel in London before working at many of the best kitchens in the country, including Wentworth Club, Sopwell House and Luton Hoo hotels.

He then trained at Westminster Kingsway College, becoming a qualified lecturer, before moving into a chef development role with Bettys and Taylors of Harrogate. He has won many cooking and BBQ competitions including Grand Champion at the British Open Freestyle BBQ Championship in 2024 and numerous gold medals at Hotelympia.

Simon is the co-founder of Hog & Beyond, a street food and BBQ company which uses Cranswick's pork and chicken to showcase local produce with global flavours at food festivals and BBQ competitions across the world – many of its BBQ recipes and techniques are found in this book.

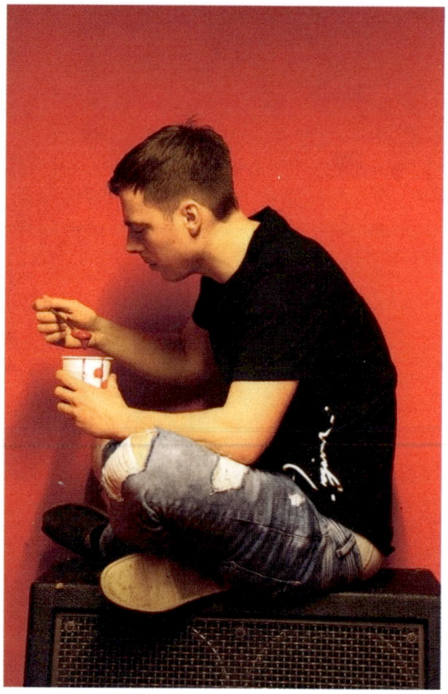

This book would not have been possible without the incredible Cranswick chefs who have contributed their talent and passion to the recipes. Each of these chefs brings a unique perspective, honed through years of experience in kitchens around the world, from traditional cooking techniques to culinary fusion. They have shared their favourite dishes, offering a glimpse into their culinary dedication. Their expertise shines through in every recipe. We're grateful for their collaboration and hard work. Their input has transformed this book into something truly special.

Top, left to right – *Ben Croydon, Jack Brooks and son Billy, Connor Berney, Alex Bolton and Ivy the terrier, Dan Allen and Neave (who also works at Cranswick), Paul Robinson.*

Bottom, left to right – *Daryl Jackson, Steve Mildren, Georgie Swinson with baby Thomas and fiancée Catherine, Florentina Dumitru, Krzysztof Biedrzycki, Dan McCormack.*

CRANSWICK
Great British Taste

First published in Great Britain in 2025 by Cranswick PLC
www.cranswick.plc.uk

A CIP catalogue record of this book is available from the British Library.
ISBN 978-1-0369-0719-8

Written by Jim Brisby & Simon Woods
Additional words and editing by Annabel Gilbert and Jeannie Swales
Design and art direction by Anthony Hodgson
Photography by Paul Robinson
Nutritional information provided by NutriCalc
Printed and bound in China by 1010 Printing International Ltd

Produced in association with Face Publications
www.facepublications.com

thank you to all the chefs who have
Jack Brooks, Connor Berney, Dan
Steve Mildren, Georgie Swinson
Special thanks to Krzysztof Biedrzy
their authentic recipes from Poland an
tirelessly behind the scenes to bring th
brain and book title, and Ash Gilman,
and Claire Burcham for their support
yorkshiregourmet.com, for his excelle
Anthony Hodgson for his creativit